# True
## Confessions

ISBN 978-1-950034-93-2 (Paperback)
True Confessions
Copyright © 2019 Michael Fanelli

Yorkshire Publishing
4613 E. 91st St,
Tulsa, OK 74137
www.YorkshirePublishing.com
918.394.2665

Printed in the USA

# True
# Confessions

*Michael Fanelli*

TULSA

# Contents

# Acknowledgments

First and foremost, I would like to thank God for the gifts He has given me. If it wasn't for His grace, I would not be here today to tell my story.

Thank you to my mother, for she stuck by me in my darkest of times, and never turned her back on me. You still believed in me when no one else did.

I would also like to thank the one who betrayed me and yet inspired me to write this story at the same time. You know who you are. By separation from you, I was able to gain hindsight and expose many truths, including my own with my story.

Finally, I would like to thank in advance all of my readers with the hope that my true confessions can help you take a closer look at your lives, to see who and what really is important, and what ultimately matters. May everyone learn something and gain insight so that they can identify their truth in life as well.

# *Disclaimer*

Some names have been left out of this book to protect the identities of parties involved, past and present. My true confessions are true, and my story is being told by me, the author, in all its content. All the views and statements in this book are the opinions of the author and are in no way meant to challenge or offend anyone.

The readers may decide on what they see as facts or opinions, and again I thank my readers for allowing me the opportunity to use my life as an example that can serve all, and to help identify their truth in life as well.

Truly yours,
Michael Fanelli

# *Introduction*

The story before you is a true story about a time in my life when a blessing turned into a nightmare of my own doing. On February 27th, 2017, I received a true blessing in federal court, and exactly one year later, I was released into society to restart my life. The true confessions throughout this book will shed light on not just the man, but the lies, the pain, the losses, and failures of being a human being.

While I am grateful to share my story, I hope that my readers can not only feel my pain but learn from it as well. I have always wanted to share my discoveries in life and use them as a message to all and any willing to receive it. This story will also talk about my deepest regrets in life—while a newfound hope still exists for the future.

My hope is that you can identify your shortcomings in life and also see your blessings—not to take them for granted at all. In 2018, as soon as I was able to rise up again, I fell, and harder than the first time. I will not say I was a victim of my environment, but rather a victim of myself. Being honest with myself will enable me to be honest with my readers so that the truth can teach us all.

While I take you on a rollercoaster of emotions, through the highs and lows of my life, I hope you will enjoy my perspective and come to a better perspective for yourself as well. My name is Michael Fanelli, and these are my true confessions.

# CHAPTER 1

# Short Lived Blessing

On February 27th, 2018, I was released from prison to a halfway house in my home state of New Jersey. It was exactly one year from the date of my sentencing. I always and still look back on how blessed I was then, and how everything worked out at that time. I remember the day like it was yesterday. My aunt and a family friend arrived at the prison to pick me up early that morning. I was in my grey sweat suit with a net bag containing my belongings. Also, inside my bag was written material for the books I was working on while in prison.

When I was escorted to the main lobby and saw my family waiting for me, I got down on one knee and shed a tear as I thanked God for this day, a day I thought would never come. We soon left and in the car to the highway we went. I called my mother first. She was away on vacation but expected my call. It was so good to hear her voice on a regular phone. Then, I called the woman I had recently been talking to, and someone I had known for years.

The ride home was surreal and I still was processing it all. I had my aunt bring me home first to pick up some clothes for the halfway house and to grab a quick bite to eat from a local Wawa. I did so, then was off to the halfway house. When I arrived shortly thereafter, I prepared myself mentally for the next step. I was unaware of the process. It was a smooth transition. I had a phone my first day there, and the second day, I picked up my truck for my license was still good, another blessing in my life.

During my time at the halfway house, I would leave daily on 10 to 12-hour day passes to look for work or go shopping. I knew soon I would be running my own business again, so I spent time with my soon to be girlfriend and was just trying to get back to living life. Most days I would pick up my girlfriend around 9am and spend till 5pm with her then drop her off on my way back to the halfway house where I had to be by 8pm each night. This went on for at least two months until I was released on home confinement on April 25th, 2018.

Backing up some, the very first time I saw her was at her brother's funeral, the first two days we met. Then we thought it was God that brought us together by timing and fate, because immediately upon my release I made it just in time to be there for her. We became close super-fast, and after just 10 days of dating, we made it Facebook official as boyfriend and girlfriend. My family was against it and felt it was way too soon to get involved with anyone, but I was happy, and soon to be in love, thinking all was well.

It was a happy time for me, and I think at first for her too. We were in the honeymoon stage and we spent most of our days joking, laughing, cuddling, making love, and just getting to know one another. Once I was home, I immediately started back up my power washing business and things were going great. It was as if I never left. After nearly three years I was gaining ground quickly with old and new customers. I felt like God was still with me, leading the way and nothing could go wrong.

It wasn't long before I was mistaken. So here I was, free, I had my family back, my business, a new girl, and was hopeful for my future. Day to day I was enjoying things as they came. I started fishing on the lake I lived on with her, for it was one of her childhood hobbies. We had fun, and I caught some decent size fish as a beginner. On weekends every Friday after work around 5pm I would pick her up at her parent's house and prepare to spend our weekends together. At first, it was good.

I would order out every weekend once I started making good money. Italian takeout and often Chinese food- whatever the princess wanted as I referred to her then. It seemed to be going well, though we had our arguments as well. Over what? You would think a new couple would not argue at all, but unfortunately it wasn't the case for us. Years before, I was a different man, a womanizer if you will. This time around I was loyal and loving, too much so that it hurt me more than it helped me.

I didn't see it then, but I overlooked red flags in our relationship that were indicators that something was wrong. Like our disputes over…what else? Facebook. I believed that in our committed relationship, we shouldn't add new people to our networks, like new women for me and new men for her. She strongly disagreed and always had her excuses why it was okay. I was 38 at the time. She was 40 already with children so you would think I would have been enough for her, sadly I was not. I put up with it. I had little choice and slowly our relationship began to deteriorate.

It wasn't long before the next bombshell would drop on me. Right after Memorial Day, her behavior would change towards me- ups and downs with affection, even shutdowns where she would not speak to me for days. Those who knew her, including her family told me this was normal for her. I thought it was crazy and was definitely not used to it. Sometime in the late June after my 39$^{th}$ birthday, the news came- she was suddenly pregnant!

Can you imagine? I was home not even four months and learned I was about to be a father. Still, I was so excited. After all we talked about having a baby, and she wanted another child too. The first time we met, back at the funeral, she held a newborn child and looked at me with a big smile and said, "I want one." What could I say, I smiled and thought it was cute. Here I was, months later, just getting my feet wet in life and now everything had changed.

It all happened so fast, and now I began practicing for amateur father of the year award. I say that because from here on out I ran around like a madman catering to her every need, any time of day or night. I was distracted at work, so I would come home early to check on her and the baby. I was so in love at this time. So, I thought. We were planning on getting married and about to get our own house together, which we set a date for October 2018. My aunt was at her shore summer home the entire time, so we had the house all to ourselves, and we took full advantage of it, playing house of our own.

It started out so good, but now with her pregnant, it became worse. Her attitude toward me sucked, put politely. She was irritated often, and I thought it was the hormones of a pregnant woman. So, I tried to comfort her in any way I could. When I was putting in so much effort and not receiving it in return, this is when I became depressed, and it began to fall apart.

Soon, I started to gamble. Not long after, the addiction that led me to prison the first time came back even stronger. I admit this—I lied about it to everyone, not just her. Instead of being honest with my family, whom I barely saw because I was so focused on her, I tried to save face and make them all believe I had everything under control. This was a huge mistake. I regret it daily. So, the more pregnant she became, the more distant she got. I was a mental wreck. I would call her brother, my longtime friend, every night for advice on how to handle her.

He tried to give me help, and even advised I walk away from her, even before she was pregnant, and the family knew. To no avail. I didn't listen, and I thought I could save us, so I stayed. I didn't want my first child to be born without two loving parents so I did what I could to continue a relationship that was sinking. On Sunday's, I would go to church with her parents, and she rarely joined us, after introducing me to that congregation.

Still, my pride got in my way. I was the guy who had written three powerful books, and had the ability to save her, so I thought at that time. In the final days of our relationship before my blessing turned nightmare we were not doing well together. Newly found parents are supposed to be excited and help each other. She practically did nothing but lay around the house, playing on her phone and watching TV. Meanwhile, I was her servant ready to jump for her at any given moment.

To recap, I was home roughly five months now, and I was under pressure to provide us a house to live in, help get her a car, and a newborn on the way. A lot for any man, especially one who just came home from prison. I was yet to experience life again, and life hit me like a ton of bricks. The last day I saw her was at a local public pool where she was swimming with her children. I was on the verge of a breakdown due to my current losses due to gambling. I wanted to confide in her, but was afraid to be honest, so I lied and said my father was sick.

Her reaction that day when I showed up at the pool was like I was a bother to her, and she had no time for me. She had been there a few hours, and one would think she would have said come on kids let's wrap it up, due to what I would call urgent and just want to be there to comfort me in my time of need. After all, I had been there for her since day one, from her brother's funeral to current day. She would not do the same for me. She asked me to leave, and she said to call her later that night around 7pm.

As I walked away, dumbfounded, she backstroked as if she had not a care in the world. At this moment, I realized truly how selfish she was, and especially after all I had done to please her. That evening she called e around 6:30pm and would you believe she began to interrogate me as to why I had shown up there without calling her first. Even when we were getting along, she barely would answer her phone for me. I would never treat her the same way. The phone call lasted a few minutes, and she hung up on me.

I could not believe her behavior and was so depressed. That was the last time we spoke on an outside telephone. The next morning would be my blessing turned nightmare. The morning of August 7th, 2018 was sunny and warm as a normal summer day. Usually I would wake up around 7am and load my truck for work, stopping over my sister's house for just next door to run with her dog before I left for work. This morning was different. As I pulled out of the driveway, my sister yelled my name, "Michael." I never looked her way. I kept going. What I didn't realize then was that it was my sign to stop and let my family know what was going on with me. I didn't.

As I drove off, it was this day on August 7th, 2018 I was about to make the biggest mistake of my life. Driving without a real plan, I tried talking myself out of what I was about to do. The should of, would have, could have would haunt me later. Around 11am, in Ardmore, Pennsylvania I walked into a local bank and committed bank robbery. This was the same crime I just served time for in federal prison and I was in shock before, during and seconds after I was doing it.

Instead of breaking the truth to my family, that I was suffering again from my gambling addiction, and had lost nearly all the money I had saved for my new family, I made this terrible decision to steal and try to cover the lie I was living. It would not work. Minutes after the robbery, while driving on 76 East back towards Philadelphia, state police vehicles began following me. I thought, how could this be? I became extremely paranoid. Being high on cocaine did not help, for shortly after I started gambling, I also began using coke to take the edge off of life.

My first thought was that someone had gotten my license plate number and reported me, but that wasn't the case. Minutes later, sirens went off. Scared, I kept driving at a moderate speed as to keep up with traffic that day. When the police were just two cars directly behind me, I was then convinced they were following me and was thinking it was all over. Up ahead at a traffic stop, it appeared to be a roadblock for a large tractor trailer was slightly turned in order to block a lane change. I veered to the far left and stopped. Within seconds, armed police officers swarmed my vehicle and shouted commands at me in all directions.

At one point, I even reached to put the truck in gear and thought they are going to shoot me. God must still love me, because I am alive to tell my story. An officer quickly opened the driver-side door, pulling me from the truck and placing me on the ground, arresting me. Inside the truck, they found everything. The mask, the money, and the toy gun I used during the crime. I was devastated and began thinking about my baby first. I was in total disbelief, and once placed inside the cop car, I was thinking that my life was over.

The police stood me up, facing the highway as a car slowed down to look at me. It was the bank teller making a positive identification on me, and that was that. I was taken to the local police station in lower Merion township P.A. After being processed in the jail,

I was locked in a cell for hours waiting for my notice for bail, if any. I was on federal probation, and knew it was near impossible. Hours later I was woken up and had video court in front of a local district judge who said, "One million dollars." For bail. I was shocked. This was the second time in my life I was a million-dollar man. Years before my bail was 1.3-million dollars for multiple robberies. It made sense then, this time I thought I was cooked.

At the station, I called my girlfriend petrified to tell her. When she answered, she thought I was lying, all I could do was apologize and saw sorry to her. Her last words to me that day were how could you do this to your pregnant girlfriend in a nasty tone, then hung up on me. I was so ashamed and then called my poor mother. When she asked me where I was calling from, she too said, "Are you for real?" I again apologized and it was a short call. Soon after I was transferred to the Montgomery County Correctional Facility in Eagleville, P.A.

It was over. The five months I was home seemed like a weekend furlough and had gone so fast. My blessing that I had worked so hard for and was given was wasted. At this time, I was so hard on myself, and was in a deep state of depression. I could not believe I was back in jail and facing another possible 10-year prison sentence. How could I let this happen? Why did I put this woman before my family, before myself, and worse, before God? It was truly my downfall. I was only 10 days in jail when she stopped taking my calls and began to erase me from her life.

I was placed on suicide watch due to emotional phone calls with my family, and the jail was concerned I was going to harm myself. That was the hardest time of my life. While I was naked in a cell, on 24-hour watch, I was deprived of a shower twice for five days at a time. Then the next big bomb would be dropped on me one night when I managed to make one short phone call to my mother. She broke the news to me and said, she lost the baby, and had a miscarriage. I was so shocked I became numb.

After that phone call, I was returned to my cell naked, cold, and all alone to deal with the loss of my first child. I will never forget it as long as I live. Weeks later, after being let out of medical and placed back into a normal housing unit, I tried calling her, but she would never answer. In late September, I gave up, and to this day never tried calling her again. It was heartless and cruel. All I wanted to do was apologize and wish her well, and never got the chance.

I was calling her brother every week, sometimes three or four times, to relay messages back and forth. It was useless and cost me hundreds of dollars. I could not believe how someone I was about to marry and take care of could just drop me like that, even though I made this huge mistake, it still seemed heartless of her. Finally, I gave up calling him in late October and the months that soon followed, she called on one occasion and texted others to my mom. Only to bring up senseless stuff, like who I confided in, and knew about my gambling. Also, to badmouth me some more.

As if my poor mother didn't have enough to deal with already. I began to mourn, and this was the time in late October I decided to return to God. As this book is written, I am still renewing my faith, and getting stronger and only through the grace of God was able to get over her. So, my blessing only lasted a short time, and as I wait for another, I am focused on those who love me, and God first and foremost. In the chapters that will follow, I will speak of my pain, losses, deepest regrets, and hope for an uncertain future. After serving just two and a half years, having my life back, my family, my business, and what looked to be a bright future, I lost it all again! This was my short-lived blessing.

CHAPTER 2

# *The Great Betrayal*

In life, it is often that people will kick you while you are down, especially when you are helpless or defenseless. For me, being in jail and having to hear people talk and point fingers from a distance was hard at first, simply because I didn't have a voice to defend myself. Later, I thought about it and came to this conclusion: who are they to judge? How quick are people at times to point at someone else's shortcomings while being oblivious to their own faults?

The Bible teaches us not to rejoice when our enemy falls or stumbles, Proverbs 24:17. Then, I said to myself, well not everyone follows God or looks at life in the spiritual light. So, was I going to let this deter me, or inspire me? It came down to a simple choice. I fell, but with God's help, I was going to get right back up.

So, while other people were badmouthing me, and sharing their pointless opinions about me, I was seeking the truth. To make matters worse, before I could do find it, I was in a deep state of depression due to the loss of my first child with my ex-girlfriend by miscarriage. While she broke up with me and deserted me just two weeks into my jail term, someone else decided it was their turn to dump on me as well.

My former fiancée, and girlfriend of five years, who had contacted me the first day I was home, had to share her comments too.

I mean, why not, right? I was locked up, what could I do about it? I could not call her, defend myself or even ask her why she was contacting my new girlfriend. Regardless, she went on to bash me and speak of the bad times in our previous relationship, and to accomplish what? I haven't asked her, and never will, simply because it plays no purpose in my future.

The ironic thing about here was, she wanted to come and visit me again. To spend a weekend with me and reunite. I first considered it, then decided against it because I did not want to be unfaithful to my current girlfriend. When I cancelled on her, she was upset. So, one can assume for her, this was payback. Through a friend I was told for days she sent books worth text messages condemning me, yet, kick me some more while I was down.

When I first heard the news, I was upset and disappointed and wanted to defend myself. This was the pride stage. I quickly moved on from pride, with prayer and the grace of God, I let it go. For I could do nothing about it anyway, so why let it take up space in my head, for I had enough on my plate to deal with. I call this a great betrayal because while I was dating my new girlfriend and we seemed to be happy, my ex would regularly talk bad about her and try to convince me to leave her.

She might have had her own agenda behind it, but she said it was for my benefit and called her trash. She told me I could do better, and deserved better, after I vented to her about some of our troubles. Later, my venting would be used against me as if I did something wrong, and I was the one guilty of betrayal. So, instead of trying to relight a flame from my past, and start over with her, I decided to stick with what was in front of me and choose a fresh start. The simple truth was that I was doomed from the beginning.

Sparing all the details, there were many irritating traits that my new girlfriend was demonstrating. What she called normal, I was dealing with for the first time in any relationship I had ever been in. So, while I was trying to compromise, it wasn't enough. Betrayal was going on regularly. I will share a short story about that later in the chapter. Still, as I sit in prison, I can only imagine what some might say about me, and how things turned out after my release and short-lived blessing.

To be betrayed, especially when you know you truly love someone, not only hurts, but leaves scars. These scars must be dealt with in order for both parties to heal and not drag their pain into future relationships. I am working on that pain, while I doubt she will. Simply because of her track record with men, since the divorce of her first husband up until me. There was so much emotional damage there, it sabotages any real chance of happiness for her, or any brave soul willing to be with her.

I am only speaking my truth. I was locked up on August 7th, 2018, and August 16th was the last time we spoke. After planning a marriage, a life together, a baby on the way, house shopping, engagement ring shopping, car shopping, and catering to her daily for five months, this is what I received: deletion. My pictures were removed as if I never existed at all from her most important Facebook page. The one she swore she barely went on, but spent more time on there looking for attention from others, when I gave her more than one man could possibly give. Then she relayed messages to her brother and my mother to never contact her again without ever speaking to me directly, even after we lost our child together. When you think about all this, it's simple math. Who was betrayed? I will take credit for getting arrested and leaving her out there. That's my truth. Sadly, I doubt and at this point stopped caring if she will ever take credit for her faults or even work on them.

The greatest betrayal here was to myself. I made promises to God, my family, and myself when I was first in prison. I worked diligently on books I wrote and spent most of my time helping others while it was also therapeutic for myself.

In doing all this, I forgot to focus on the one person who needed it the most, me. I put more effort into chasing a girl I couldn't reach rather than myself and all the goals I was trying to accomplish. I wind up losing everything in the process. While again, I can't directly blame her, she was of no help to my cause, and simply, selfishly only cared about herself. When the finance was gone, so was the romance. She even had the nerve to lie to my mother and ask for the last few thousand I had, saying it was her money, so my mom could give it to her.

I am glad my mother was smart enough not to believe her lies, for she would have taken my last dollar and left me anyway. Some people are just evil. From here I will reflect on not just one betrayal, but any that has hindered me in life from making an everlasting change. I learn a lot about people and myself every day, and more importantly the sad part of life is that people are going to let us down, time and time again. This is why I place my hope, and trust in God.

There will be lies spread about us, people who will betray us, and leave us in our darkest moments. This brings about my newest quote: Don't define me by what's behind me. My past will only play a part in my future for teaching purposes, so that I will not make the same mistakes again. We are all imperfect and there is always room for improvement. As this book continues, you will find that I am releasing my pain first in my true confessions, so that I can heal, as well as help my readers see that we all have to heal first before we can see the truth clearly.

This is my great betrayal.

# CHAPTER 3

# Know Your Place

Growing up, I remember most of my childhood wanting to be a baseball player or a wrestler. As I got older, I looked up to my dad, and he became my closest role model. It was easy, because he could be found right at home, and I could watch his every move and learn from him. Years later, I would want to be nothing like my father and for several reasons. In life, we can easily become confused and become lost. We also do this in relationships with one another and sometimes put people in a box as to how we see them, and what we can expect from them.

This is wrong, and is a great reason to become let down, especially by the ones we love and are closest to. I always had this image of my father as a successful businessman, who could do no wrong. For a time, he was indeed successful, at least financially. Money is not the only part of success, in fact, it is just a by-product of it, or simply put, the icing on the cake. For me, I would rather have the cake itself without a sugarcoated icing, and here is why. The icing is designed to draw us in, and entice us, when the actual real substance is the cake itself.

The cake is the foundation in all of our relationships, yet we become distracted by the outer appearance of others, or the icing, that we lose focus on the substance. In my most recent relationship, I saw this over and over. My expectations of that person were far greater than who she was as a person, and how she saw her behaviors.

This is why the Bible again teaches us to not be unequally yoked. If two cannot agree, how can they agree?

This story is another one of my true confessions. One day while at a local public lake, my girlfriend, her son and I were fishing. Without notice, she randomly walked up to a strange man who was fishing across the lake and asked him for a lure that we did not have. Mind you, it was summer, and she was dressed in short clothing, with her breasts nearly out in her summer tank top. I was upset—to be polite—and when she came back to where I was fishing with her son, I asked her why she did what she did. Her reply was that we are fishermen, and that this is what we do. As a man, and I am sure most will agree it made me look foolish and would be wondering, what could that guy be thinking about it? Regardless, it was disrespectful to me, and when I confronted her about it, she said, "Well, he had something you didn't have that I needed." I was blown away and thought, so that's who you are?

I think it would be safe to believe that any time you need something from someone, you will completely disregard the person you are committed to, and just do your own thing. That day did not end well, and we parted ways early. When I vented this to another woman, to get a woman's perspective, she replied, "I would never. That was rude, disrespectful to you, and to herself." This girl clearly doesn't know her place. If she would have asked me to go over to the stranger it would have been different, but being the flirt that she was, and used to doing whatever she wanted her whole life, she saw nothing wrong with what she did. It was the first of many red flags to come in this relationship.

What struck me later on was that the person I was dating was a Christian, yet her behavior was revealing to me that she did not practice Bible scripture in her everyday life. We were not married, but were planning on it, and it clearly states that wives should submit to their husbands, and husbands to their wives. I would never have walked up to a strange female in front of her especially and struck up a conversation without notice to my significant other. I was beginning to realize that I could never tame this woman and wasted a great deal of my time trying to.

The problem with people in most relationships is that we do not know our place. Not just to our partner, but to ourselves. We become so caught up in life that we don't take notice of things that we actually do that can affect others as well as ourselves. While I doubt she will ever care about what I say, speaking my truth, this is why most people end up alone, or in bad relationships. Respect is so important if you want to be respected. Once you make a commitment to someone, you give up your single habits and have to respect your partner, as they also have to respect you.

I once dated a woman who had 60 friends on Facebook and she said, 'These are my friends and family.' I believed her and thought she was honest. That's what this website was created for initially, but today it is a platform for selling us what we don't need, gathering our information to profile us, and frankly causes more harm and damage to relationships than it does good. It constantly puts in our face how many choices or options are out there, distracting us from the person in front of us, at least to those who allow it to.

To men and women out there, unless your significant other is an international businessman or woman and using social media as a work platform, beware. If they have 2,000 to 5,000 friends, they just might be superficial looking for others to validate them. This was the case in my relationship. Note to self, my next relationship will not be with any woman who spends more than 30 minutes a day on social media. While it can be a useful tool, it is also a hammer that drives a nail right between people and the devil is working at his finest hour.

It really is sad that with all the educational books, and Internet resources that we have available to us today, most people are concerned with who likes their picture, and sharing every move of their life with strangers they call friends. I also fell victim to this, and no longer will place it above my priorities or goals in life. First, being faithful to God. Then spending quality time with my family. Finally, being true to myself, and living God's purpose for my life.

Looking back through the stages of my life, I too often lost my place. I tried to be something that I wasn't and lost myself while doing so. It again brings me to Bible scripture: do not be pleasers of men, rather in all things please God. This is so true, I must confess.

When we live our purpose in life, the one that is for us, and not others. We are not only happier, but we are better people all around for others as well.

At first, when I started writing this book, I had to revise a lot, simply because my walk is becoming more and more spiritual. I am seeing things from a new perspective, a higher view. A view that can only speak truth for everyone, but as I unveil my confessions in each chapter, I will leave you with some inspiration in hopes that you too can see things clearer and know your place in yourself, so that you can live a more meaningful and productive life.

We must all know our place, and especially not box others in or allow them to box us in. To think outside the box, you have to live outside the box, and when doing so, not lose sight of who you are and what your purpose in life is. For what hurts today, may better us tomorrow. I know God is chastising me for my good, because he loves me. Love yourself so that you can, not only live your best life possible, but also to be happy and confident that you know your place.

I've had to make a lot of mistakes in order to learn my place and what I thought I wanted to be, is nothing compared to who God wants me to be. Through His love and grace, I have found my path. I pray for all those who have yet not and encourage them to find it. Time can teach us many things. It exposes so much truth, even when some may try to cover it with lies. The truth makes you feel better even if it is something you don't want to hear. It remains the same—it never changes—unlike lies that you have to constantly tell one to cover another, adding more icing. Learn to enjoy a plain cake and see substance for what it truly is. "Know your place." I thank her for this inspiration, for this is just another lesson I had to learn, and another of my true confessions.

# CHAPTER 4

# Save Yourself

When I came home from prison, March 2018, I had a goal. I was strong and ready to take on the world with my plans. Working hard for nearly the last three years, I felt ready as ever, and I was confident I could do so. The thing I never saw coming was that I would try to please one person above all others and try to save someone who wasn't ready to be saved. Looking back, I see a guy who tried to be a knight in shining armor, riding into town on a white horse, ready to save the day.

When I met my ex-girlfriend, she asked me—due to the recent struggles in life and what seemed, at the time, to be making progress to making peace with my past demons—if I could help her with her demons. Maybe, I could help her to stop resenting her past and the anger it still caused her after all she'd been through, but I was all too eager to take on the task, causing me to fail miserably. I failed because I still was battling my greatest demon, a gambling addiction. I didn't know it then, but it was still dormant and ready to explode.

When I tried to help her, she shut down on me. Any time I would confront her about anything, she had no time for it. All she wanted was peace. Unfortunately, in any relationship, there will be conflicts, and without addressing them appropriately, they will simply not go away. I tried explaining this to her and it was a project. Still, due to my ego and the love I had for her, I wasn't ready to give up yet. Throughout the time we dated, many issues sprouted.

Time after time, I got the same results, "Leave me alone, I don't like confrontation."

What she didn't understand was I was only trying to help. How can any couple work through problems without talking? It was like talking to a wall. Eventually, it all got so bad that there were periods of her shutting down for weeks at a time. Then we would hang out again, as if nothing had ever happened. This was so unhealthy, destroying us more than we knew. First off, our views on life were different. The only thing we seemed to want was a family and to settle down, although, I believe, her actions prove otherwise.

You see, just because you spend a lot of time with someone, doesn't mean you are actually there with them. Her body was present, but at times, her mind was elsewhere. I would come home from work and immediately be excited to run into the house and see her. Most of the time she was playing on her phone like a teenager, not excited to see me at all. The worst feeling ever is when your partner does not show you love in return. It makes you question yourself, that person, and makes you feel inadequate. This was the case for me. I was entering a battle I was not prepared for, and in the end, it consumed me.

When I was going to church, and she would not join, I thought, "You introduced me to this congregation, and now you never show up." Later, when I was in jail, she started going regularly with her parents, which was a slap in the face to me. Though I imagine it was to please her parents and keep the peace at home, now that I wasn't there to rescue her and get her a home of her own. She needed them again, for I was out of the picture. Even her brother agreed with me at this point.

Regardless of why she did what she did, or what she does now, this much is true. I tried to save her, when I should have saved myself. I allowed my co-dependency on her to blind me from the truth, and ultimately, it tore me away from my goals, and even my own family—one of my biggest regrets. I played Superman in the past, only this time, my cape was torn, my wings were broken, and she was broken long before I came into the picture. I tried to save a broken bird, and in turn I lost myself.

I learned a lot from this experience, though I am going through many trials and tribulations being incarcerated once again. Here is what I find: maybe she wasn't ready for that congregation, or maybe I wasn't the one who was meant to save her. Her parents told me, on one occasion, I was the best thing to happen to her in years. In fact, she felt that she had a purpose again, other than her kids. She had a really strange way of showing it. I have little doubt that she will move on fast, or even get anywhere fast because of her problem—a void in her that still exists.

These things just don't go away on their own, they take effort along with time. Maybe I didn't have enough time, but while she was spared from that congregation, I was spared from her! God is good! There is a reason for everything, and though I wish her well, despite all that has happened to me, I wonder often if she ever really loved me, misses the man and not just the lifestyle that I brought. Today, my main focus is on God and His plans for me.

I, as we all should, focus on myself first, so as not to be lost by trying to save someone else. We cannot give things people are not willing to receive, no matter how hard we try. I tried to save her, in essence, I lost myself. Helping others is a great thing, only if it doesn't hurt you in the process. I learned from all this and I hope all of you can learn from my mistakes as well. While reaching for your goals and putting your best foot forward, please, always remember to first save yourself.

CHAPTER 5

# In My Own Way

I believe the worst pain anyone can ever suffer from is one that is self-inflicted. This brings me to my story of failure by means of standing in my own way. Most of my life, I was lost, trying to find who I was. During these times of my life, I made many mistakes and took on many alter-ego's, sometimes even believing I could live a double life and make ends meet. After being in prison again, and taking a closer look at my past, I can see this: a man who continued to stumble by trying to always please others at the expense of himself.

Not only in this form, but many others. The well-known definition of insanity is this: doing the same thing over and over again and expecting a different result. For me this is madness. Almost every gift I received I wasted, never putting it to good use. Most of all, fear of change, along with fear of failure, has caused me to stumble in ways that have dramatically altered my life into what it is today. My biggest downfall to date is my gambling addiction, I believe. It began in my early twenties and has gotten over the years.

Countless times, I struggled to stay afloat, even going completely broke three times. Somehow, I managed to get back on my feet. This was all throughout my twenties up into my thirties. That's when the best thing happened to me. I discovered my talent to sell and produce quality work, too. My first small business was power washing. To date, I love my business. It allowed me to connect with people from different backgrounds and taught me how to build good character. I made great money, worked for myself, with low overhead, and made full time pay from a seasonal business. This afforded me a lot of free time to myself, which hurt me more than it helped—thanks to some of the choices I've made.

Spring, summer, and fall, I worked hard and saved for the winter. When the winter would come, though, I would gamble away most of what I worked for all year. This left me depressed and angry at the world. Only it wasn't the world's fault, it was my own doing, and I became disgusted with myself, and of standing in my own way. After losing everything, due to my addiction and crimes in 2015, I was incarcerated with a three-year sentence. This was a miracle and a blessing I would soon destroy. Standing in my own way has become such a habit that it has gone subtly unnoticed until now.

I've held several promising jobs in the past, but I always managed to screw things up. Running around with multiple women, drinking and gambling. Needless to say, making memories that would amount in nothing to show for today. I went on and off medications, trying to medicate my problems. I sometimes went for patient therapy, too, trying to talk out my issues, but nothing seemed to work. At times, it seemed hopeless. I somewhat accepted this as who I was, thinking I was okay with it and I'd be fine. I was very wrong. When an addiction lays dormant and is not addressed, it only comes back stronger. For me, a living nightmare was about to unfold.

While in prison—the last time—I wrote three inspirational books, putting much effort into each of them. My life story, along with self-help motivational material, which helped many men in my prison compound, myself included. When I came home, I threw my bag of books in the closet, and they still sit there today, collecting dust. This was not my intended goal. I lose and I lose due to my poor decisions. Over the course of the last 15 years, I have lost two finances, my freedom and businesses (twice, each), all my savings, and my first child.

All this loss, and for what? A gambling addiction. I think about this daily, and I see the gambling as a severe symptom of my problem, opposed to the problem itself, me! All of my life, I've tried to be someone I'm not, or something I'm not, and I'm tired of it. I can honestly say, I just want to be me. Not just me, but the best me possible. Standing in my own way doesn't have to be the way my story ends, and I refuse to let it.

Back in prison, with an uncertain future at this point, I am hopeful. I am working on the source of problem and digging deeper than ever. Here is what I have discovered: I am done trying to prove to my father I am a man. Also, instead of trying to prove to everyone else, including myself, that I am, "The man." It's time to just be a man. I owe that much to myself, God, and those who love me, especially my mother, who has been there for me through thick and thin. At some point in all of our lives, we reach that point and simply say, "Enough is enough."

My biggest inspiration comes from God, and Bible teachings on how we are supposed to live our lives. Though we are all human, and imperfect, we can all make improvements. Proverbs specifically tells us how to live our lives, and I see how much it works in everyday situations that I am arriving at now in my life. This is because I am paying attention, rather than letting life happen as it has. A famous quote from the movie A Bronx Tale, featuring Robert DeNiro, rings bells for me: the saddest thing in life is wasted talent. God has given us all gifts, and knowing what mine are, and how blessed I am, I will not waste them any longer, for life here on Earth is short.

I am exhausted to say the least, I am sick and tired of standing in my own way! So many times in life, people are just around the corner from real success, and they fail due to fear of doubt, or even what others will think of them. We cannot allow ourselves to think this way, or to be placed in a box by ourselves or others. This is all too common, and a great deal of my failures, at least, speak loudly from my fears of these things.

I am not saying that fear is not common, but it should not determine the outcome of our lives. For too long, it has shifted my life and lead me to terrible places that I no longer wish to arrive at. The change has to happen now, and it is long overdue. All of my life, I've depended on me to solve all my problems, and temporary fixes lead to falls. A quick fix is only masking the problem, and no real solution can be found by it.

While other people can stand in our way at times, doubting us, not supporting what we want to achieve, there is no greater damage than standing in your own way. Imagine tripping over your own feet every day, and falling further and further back in life. Tell me this is not insanity! It is not the design of the shoes we wear, but the roads that we travel with those shoes that make up where we will end up.

As for myself, I am tired of living with regrets from mistakes that I've made, by poor choices, and worrying about how I can please others. The void in my life that I have tried to fill, all along, it was wrong. I was looking for another person or material thing to fill it. I believed if I had a lot of money, then I was successful. If I had a beautiful woman, it completed me. While these things are nice and appear enticing on the outside, they could never meet my needs on the inside.

Instead of looking for God to send me things or give me someone to complete me, it was right in front of me all along. My completion in Jesus Christ. We cannot take anything with us when we leave this earth, and what we leave behind is our good name, so we hope. The peace I am achieving today, and continue to seek, is found in God. He has been the one to lift me up in my darkest hours, even after I lost everything, I thought that mattered.

He hasn't pointed his finger at me, rather, He extended His mighty hand to pull me up. I never deserved this grace I am receiving but am grateful to have it. While I will continue to work on myself in all areas, I truly hope this chapter has shed some light on all those who have read it. So much more can be accomplished in our lives if we humble ourselves and learn to duck sometimes, or, simply put, stand in our own way.

I have been blessed with many gifts. Blessed with a loving family above all, a God who forgives me, and has given me a talent to express myself with honesty. I am learning most importantly how to be content with what little I have so I can better be prepared for all I will receive one day. Whether it's in this lifetime, or the next. One thing for sure, I am moving forward, while pausing from time to time to listen, and for my own good. To never again let anything distract me, defeat me, especially myself, by standing in my own way.

<head>CHAPTER 6</head>

# *My Deepest Regrets*

In this life, we will all face some sort of loss, and go through disappointment from time to time. People will let us down, our expectations of others will not be met, and we will feel hurt by this. For me, my deepest regrets are self-made and cut deep. Since childhood, I have been making mistakes that, soon after, I would regret. Today, I look back on some of those regrets, and reflect on them. One of my biggest, to date, is that almost at 40 years old, I am yet to become a father and have a family of my own.

I had a chance most recently, before my incarceration, and I lost it. It often tears me apart, and I tell myself there is still hope, for I will be home again one day and will have the chance again. I was so excited to learn that after years of partying, clubbing, and fooling around with women, finally I was settling down and ready to have a child, get married, and have a family of my own.

As soon as it came, it went. A short three months I ran around doing what I could to comfort my then girlfriend and be the best dad I could possibly be. No one could dispute that. Soon after, I was arrested for a crime and lost all that I was building, including them, my soon to be family. She left me almost immediately, and soon after, we lost our baby by miscarriage. It broke my heart when I heard the news, and we never spoke again, not by my choice.

Moving on, again I lost the business that I loved, and I started from the ground up by myself. A second time I came home, and as if I had never left, got the business running again and was making money hand over fist. In four months, I had a larger savings account than the average American. I was so blessed, and I regret this also. One of my biggest regrets is a promise I made to my mother, and to God. I let them both down, for I swore I would never return to prison, and make the same mistakes.

I failed because I failed myself. I never took proper steps to get help, for my gambling addiction, and unfortunately, it led me back to prison. Another big regret I have is the big loss of time I will now have in regard to my family, the people who stuck with me through everything in my life. The time I spent with them during my short time home, was a disgrace. I put a woman, who wasn't my wife, before everyone and everything, and I regret that the most.

There were so many things I wanted to do with my family, and I pray every day that soon I will have that chance to do so. I think of my mother, who for a time, was so proud of me, and I let her down in a big way. I could have trusted her enough to let her know what was going on with me. I could have prevented all of this from happening.

This is something that has haunted me for quite some time now. It brought me to my knees before God, to bring me peace over it, and to learn to forgive myself. One of my deepest regrets is the three books I wrote while I was in prison the first time, now sitting, collecting dust in my closet. I worked so hard and was so focused for nearly three years, then tossed all of my goals, hard work, and ambition to the floor once I was home.

As I write this book, my fourth, still, I look forward to organizing my first book and publishing it, so that I can share it with who it was intended for. I often wonder about turning 40, what will life be like when I return home? Will I have the chance to find a good woman? Have the traditional family that I always wanted? Is this a milestone age in my life? One for which I should be building security for my future and real structure on a foundation?

This weighs heavy on my heart, and with this I pray for another miracle and another chance, at a young age, to once again—and for good—to start my life over. My vows to God that I was so firm about, cut me deep to my soul. God has blessed me so much, and though I know I can never repay him, I want to do my part using my talent to help others and give back to my community in any way I can.

I want to make a difference in the world, and at times, I felt like I was doing just that, even just by servicing my customers with my business. Especially my senior citizens who always commended me on a fine job, with great work, and most importantly, they trusted me. Being honest means so much, and my honor in business was an image I swore to uphold. Even after my first term in jail, old customers welcomed me back and did not judge me, another true gift from above. I feel like I let them down in a big way, and I miss my business a great deal.

Most men come from prison and struggle to find work due to lack of experience or their criminal record. This never stopped me, and I was achieving some success right away, at least financially with my business. The loss of my business a second time is a deep regret, and I hope to regain it again someday. With so much loss, it brings me to the next area in my life of failed relationships. This is a big area of failure in my life, for I should have been married twice, and a father three times—something I am far from proud to list as a regret.

It seems like every time I get ready to settle down and start a real life with someone, I screw up or something goes wrong. Throughout my twenties and early thirties, I was unfaithful to most of my girlfriends, and usually this was the cause of my failed relationships. Another big cause of everything was my gambling addiction. It drove wedges between my significant others and myself. One of my all-time biggest regrets was the loss of who you could say was the love of my life, Sarah.

Sarah and I met in Montreal, Canada, back in 2010. I was living up there with my father, trying to rebuild my life at that time and running from my problems back home in New Jersey. Namely, this was my gambling addiction and Atlantic City itself. I thought, if I could run far enough away, so could my problems. It seemed to work for a time, but later proved false.

Getting back to my relationship, Sarah was a sweet girl—my greatest companion. We could have fun together doing anything, just sitting around the house, watching movies, whatever. When unfortunate events required me to return to the United States, she packed her bags and followed me. We were living together in my aunt's house, which started out okay, but soon turned into a disaster. Due to financial problems for me, and not having my own place, Sarah was forced to return to Canada with a promise to return once I got my life in order.

Still, we couldn't stay away from each other. For the next year, she would make weekend trips back and forth by bus to visit me, and we would Skype often during the downtime of us being apart. It worked for a time, but I soon found myself in nightclubs, fooling around with other women to fill the void of time that I was alone. Still missing Sarah, I made many mistakes. In late 2013, I finally secured my own condo, and Sarah soon joined me, and it looked as though we were finally going to start a life together. We did immigration paperwork and were legally engaged, planning on marriage so she could stay in the U.S. with me.

During this time, though, I was still gambling on and off, going broke, getting back on my feet quickly, because this was during the time of my business. The summer of 2014 was one of the happiest times of my life. Sarah and I lived together from June until September, basically spending the whole summer together—our first real summer since 2010. It ended with a breakup that neither of us ever recovered from, really. Although, in 2015 she still made weekend trips out to see me during the summer.

I could probably write many chapters about that time, and our relationship, but I am touching on main points, moving right along to when I finally lost her for good in September of 2015—due to my arrest for bank robbery. During my incarceration, Sarah would often correspond with me through the prison email system. Often telling me how great her life was and how much better she was without me, as if to stick the dagger in me a little deeper. Still, I forgave her, and

I couldn't blame her for moving on. I thought I would be away for closer to ten years and could never rebuild our relationship.

My miracle happened on February 27$^{th}$, 2017, when I was sentenced to just three years in federal prison. Everyone was shocked, no one more than me, for my faith in God was greatly rewarded, and to this day haunts me. Through the email she congratulated me, and we often messaged each other. Towards the end of my sentence, I was already talking to another woman, my soon to be girlfriend, and had no intention of going backward on my life.

Today, I think I might have been better off. At least I can say Sarah did truly love me. The first day I was home, within an hour, Sarah had sent me a message via Facebook, welcoming me home with a heart emoji. I didn't respond for at least a month, due to my new relationship and out of respect. We were together for five years, lived together for two years in between, and always, for the most part, enjoyed one another's company. She said I was her soulmate, and I thought so too.

Now being locked up again, with an uncertain future, I may never get that chance to repair our relationship—at least as friends—due to my incarceration. Even worse, Sarah reached out to my newest ex-girlfriend and poured dirt on me, badmouthing me for all my mistakes against her. I guess you could say a woman scorned, but payback for not allowing her to visit me back in June of 2018 when we almost made plans to follow through with what would probably have led to many more problems.

Still, I forgive her even now, so that God may forgive me, and I don't live with the resentment for the rest of my life. I cannot, and will not, live that way. I have apologized to her many times for my past with her, all I can do is move forward from here and make the best of my life from here on. So, all that being said, to date, and I'm sure Sarah would agree, this is one of my deepest regrets and I may have lost my soulmate forever.

With so many deep regrets and losses I have endured, I am learning to let go, and not just the human relationships, but my long problem of attachment to things in general. I am focusing on God, and hoping in Him to bring forth new blessings in my life that I will not take for granted, using them properly. At the very least, in my last relationship, even though it failed, I was able to remain faithful, and that is something I will continue to practice in any relationship I may have in the future.

There is still a lot of work to be done, but we can all use improvements, right? Sure, we can! The lessons I am learning, and the pain of loss I have endured, are tremendous lessons. Losing twice my freedom, business, and fiancées, along with my first child and life savings—while some point their fingers and blame, I am searching for not only God's purpose in my life, but how best to use it, to use my life to its fullest potential and purpose.

I have made a lot of mistakes and have many regrets, these were some of my biggest and deepest ones, which inspire me to be better for myself and everyone I encounter in life. My failures will not destroy me, nor define me, but instead, spring me forward, only looking back to learn from past mistakes. I encourage all to do the same, especially if they have any deep regrets. Please, for your sake, and those you love, release them.

Holding onto regrets will only hinder us, and eventually ruin us. Progress can always be made when we learn to let go and stay positive about the future. I am using this opportunity to say I am truly sorry to anyone I have ever hurt, let down, and disappointed. Please, forgive me, and yourselves so that true peace within can be obtained. I thank God every day for my gifts, and I look forward to what He has in store for me.

Let this chapter reflect my insight on my deepest regrets, along with hope that change is possible and better days are to come.

CHAPTER 7

# *Emotionally Damaged*

This next chapter will detail some true details of a relationship I experienced with someone who was emotionally damaged and left me reeling as collateral. In relationships, often times we jump right in, not really knowing who we are dating, rather, just liking what we see on the outside. For me, this was my first big mistake. Other red flags began to appear, so when I tried to confront the problem, the person took the confrontation as an attack on them personally.

This is all too common in relationships. Whenever a problem arises in a relationship, a conflict is born. The only way to resolve the conflict is to address the problem and talk it over with your partner. When the other person involved makes excuses over and over, or shuts down to avoid the conflict, it gets old fast, and worse, sometimes never gets resolved.

This was a nightmare for me. It seemed as though the other party involved was so used to other men messing up that she was just waiting for, and expecting, me to do the same. When dating someone who thinks this way, it is a huge problem. They are so emotionally damaged that when things seem to be going right, it must be too good to be true. They are so used to things failing, or going wrong, ultimately, they tend not to know how to be treated well.

I'm not saying I was perfect by any means, but what I did wrong was allow the non-communication to continue, and chose to love her, rather than loving myself better. We must put ourselves first in situations like this, to protect ourselves from becoming lost. I lost sight of not only who I was, but also tried to save someone who wasn't willing to make a real effort to change herself. Old habits die hard and destroy most relationships.

God spoke clearly to King Solomon in the Bible saying not to go over and mess with women, for soon you will follow and worship them, not me. I made this very mistake, instead of putting God first, I followed her, and ran towards pleasing her family, forgetting my own—the very people who cared for me the most. When a person has been emotionally scarred for years, without having the proper help they need, they drag their drama into every relationship they have, the result of that relationship ending the same.

No change takes place because the person remains the same. They continue to blame others, make excuses, and look for land-mines to step on. How can any relationship work without good communication? Easy, it won't.

What happens next, we become emotionally damaged as a direct result of being exposed to the damaged person we try to care for and fix. Even more, a piece of me was still broken, which I never discussed. Together, we were a cocktail for disaster. I offered, time and time again, and was willing to go with her to see a psychologist, she "yessed" me to death, but never went. I learned so much from this relationship, even in this book. If she could ever read it one day, I hope she can be honest with herself and learn from it.

I've made my share of mistakes, but in every relationship, it takes two people to solve every problem, and I was beating a dead horse when it came to any confrontation with her whatsoever. What I have learned from this is to never lose yourself while chasing some-one who constantly runs from you instead of working with you. If two cannot communicate, how can they agree?

It is impossible for any meaningful relationship to work with-out healthy conflict and key communication between both parties. I could never have reached her because she wasn't willing to hear me. I trusted my emotions, as well as myself, to someone who was emotionally damaged long before I came along, and probably still is. Nothing will change when we are lying to ourselves and not seeking help to resolve our issues.

I can honestly say I have loved three times, and I had my heart broken three times. I guess it's just a part of life. To protect ourselves from these types of relationships, going slow with a new person would be best. Then taking time to talk with each other to see where your strong points are, and what you agree and disagree on. Jumping in with my heart and not my head has been one of my biggest downfalls in life, not just with women, but also addiction.

Before I wrote this chapter, I thought a lot about how she might be doing, then I realized it didn't matter. All that mattered was getting myself together, so when I enter the next big relationship, I am not damaged for the next person. A lot of people jump from one person to the next and never take time to heal. This is a big mistake, and it often leads to failure. While no relationship is perfect, much work is needed. Take a look to see how much work you are putting in and how much your partner is.

If you do everything, you will fail. I allowed this for months, and the result cost more than a relationship, it cost me my freedom.

We all have become victims at times of our own ways, and not allowing change to happen, because we not only fear change, and become scared by unfamiliar territory. We also fear success and even think we don't deserve it or are unworthy of a good thing. This way of thinking is wrong, and we only wind up damaging ourselves further and we lose a good thing, or possible chance at healing ourselves.

While no one person is the ultimate solution to us getting over emotional scars, we can allow them to help us, help ourselves by being honest and communicating about what we have been through and how we want things to be different this time. To experience something different we must do different things, that are beneficial to both parties, leaving no one hurt, scarred or damaged.

When someone, like she often did, puts up a wall every time things don't go their way, or as they hoped, this destroys any chance of resolution and fixing the relationship. While she ay of felt like she was teaching me a lesson by not speaking to me for a time, it hurt us both more than any good came out of it. I just wish to this day she could understand that, and seen what I saw, and how it affected us both.

Well, I learned from it, and I am sure she will always blame me, as she did all of her ex-boyfriends. It doesn't matter, the proof is in the pudding. The ugly truth about people like that is they often just don't even care about anyone but themselves, only staying emotionally damaged being the very problem that enters every relationship they engage in.

I am no psychologist, but after taking time to reflect on that entire relationship, while comparing it to many others, it's not rocket science to figure out. A person who is still alone, living home with several children in their 40's is the mother of all red flags, screaming to be careful. In my case, I should have never ignored it for what it was, or her for who she was.

We all have setbacks in life, but we will never move forward or make progress when we make no effort to change and continue to blame others for our broken lives.

Everyone deserves to be treated right, and loved. While every relationship will be different, one thing stays the same, no communication, then be prepared to fail. I truly hope this individual will get help one day for herself, before anyone else. I have done so and will never lose myself again in chasing an emotionally damaged person who can't receive my help by not giving themselves a real chance to help themselves.

After three loves and three losses, it's time to heal. This is another true confession, that I hope will help someone else and make a difference in their life before they suffer a loss like I have. I have run in wrong directions for too long, and though we all have faults I am loving myself first, as should we all, before trying to love or commit to someone else.

# CHAPTER 8

# *Saving Face*

One of my biggest regrets in life is common to many of us. Our image before other and how we appear to them. This is what I call our perception of reality. For me, I became consumed not only by my addiction, but by how others perceived me to be, instead of how I perceived myself. This mindset becomes a problem. Throughout our lives, we have all worn masks for other people. Trying to be someone we thought they wanted us to be, and then us believe if we could meet their image of us, we were then acceptable.

This is wrong and will never allow us to be who we were meant to be. How we perceive ourselves is important. Then being comfortable in our own skin. Another person's acceptance of who we are should come last, if at all. Of course, we want to please our families, friends or significant others. But when that need consumes our ability on how we should truly perceive ourselves, we enter a stage of saving face. This stage ultimately destroyed me.

When covering my failures with lies, to maintain an image of success, my perception became a false reality, blinding others to the truth, including myself. A lot of us try to save face instead of facing our problems for what they truly are. We become worried about what others will think, or say about us, and then treat us. The reality is we end up fooling ourselves and hurting others as well as ourselves, trying to hide the truth.

Saving face is our misperception of our own truth, and we are better off being honest with all parties, only then we can identify the problem we face and resolve it. My true confession is this: I thought if I succeeded in business, I was someone. If I had a beautiful girlfriend, I was "the man." These were all self-inflicted beliefs of what I thought were acceptable to those who knew me, and society as a whole. For years I dated a variety of women, thinking I was cool, a smooth operator, and the champion around my friends.

While some of my married friends wanted my lifestyle, soon after I wanted theirs. The problem is we always think the grass is greener on the other side. I say, "It's whatever color you want it to be." Our misplaced beliefs or ideas of what others see in us, is who we try to become, and it is who I became as a person before my incarceration. Today I live for God and try to be an imitator of Christ. In a fallen world, this is difficult and with character builds hope, and produces the beautiful person or creation that I, and we all are meant to be.

"No longer will I worry about pleasing others to the point of my own demise." Saving face leads to losing so much more. When we look at our lives the way we should, we see a new reality, a perception of truth, our truth, and that's what counts the most. While many people will continue looking for others or other's beliefs to complete them, I will be content with who I am, and let God complete me, so I can be who I was meant to be. Trying to save face has temporarily cost me my freedom, being able to care for those I love in person, and it has cost me my ability to be who I am for myself first, and all the privileges that come along with freedom.

It's safe to say that trying to protect my image, by saving face, cost my whole body more than I was willing to give.

Our best face is an honest one. So, if there is a problem, we can work on it. So, we can be right for ourselves, and others around us— especially those we love. I see a different person in the mirror today, because my mask of lies is off! I just see me, and it has never felt so good to be okay with just that! I am saving myself with the grace of God by identifying the problem, working on it, and staying honest above all with myself during the process.

When you are truthful with yourself it does set you free. No longer will you feel the need to wear a mask you once thought looked good for others. Save yourself, by being your best self, instead of trying to save face. Love yourself, accept yourself, and always be honest with yourself. Your perception of the truth will dramatically change, and the way you view the world will be different. For the good of yourself and others who truly care about you.

If I had only been honest with myself to be honest with my family with what was going on with me, I would not have caused myself so much more loss, and would not have caused myself so much more loss, and pain, and wouldn't of went to prison again. Lies always do more damage than good, especially when you are lying to yourself. I learned a valuable lesson with this true confession, and one that I hope all of my readers can do as well.

# CHAPTER 9

# Renewing My Faith

Sitting back in jail at FDC Philadelphia, I feel like a dog returning to its own vomit. This is stated in the Bible and feels like my reality at the moment. After all that has happened, all that I lost, and with all ahead that I will have to face, there was only one place that I could turn to, God. This wasn't easy, considering I wasn't ready to forgive myself yet. Even so, I knew that God could forgive me, but would He I asked myself? The first five months back in jail was a real struggle. A struggle with not just all that transpired, but with myself.

I realized that I had to let go, not just my fear, but all the garbage that was still inside me, polluting me, and preventing me from healing and getting back on track. Through daily Bible studies, and fellowship with other men, slowly I began to do this. I made an honest effort to look at who I was, and who I wanted to be. Then I said, but who does God want me to be? This was a deep question I was unsure of, and even now still seek to know. I believe that we grow spiritually little by little.

Things happen to build our faith, but true faith is believing even when you can't see things happening. I was in the dark until I saw little things happening that might of seemed like just luck to others. First, I wanted to have my state case dropped, and have the Feds pick up my case. I had several reasons for this agenda. Then after they picked up my case, that agenda changed. Once back in federal custody, I had just a week or so to get my mother approved again for a visit before she left town on her winter vacation.

I prayed about it, and wouldn't you know that the week of Christmas, just two days after, she was approved on my list and we had our first visit together in five months. Immediately I thought, God is good! Then I prayed I would get a cellmate that I would get along with, and that happened. A big thing was when my lawyer walked up to me in the courtroom and said you're going to be alright; everything is going to be alright, keep the faith. It was as if God was speaking to me in that very moment.

Then that same afternoon I was assigned who my federal judge would be, and my lawyer whispered in my ear: you got a good judge, he's a good judge, I know him and have dealt with him before. As I am writing this a man walked in the room where I am typing and said he has been incarcerated 22 years, but he is patiently waiting on the Lord. This was amazing to me to see his faith, for most men would have given up, or lost hope at that point. He said God is good, my reply, all the time!

That event may have been a sign for me today just to remind me that God is always in control. The thing that I, and all of us have to accept, is that we wait on His time frame for our blessings. It's hard to let go, for we are creatures who are used to instant gratification. This discipline of waiting on God molds us into better people, for ourselves and others as well. I know He can do anything but that wasn't my issue at first. My thought was: will He do it again? As mentioned in the Bible, well that was then, and this is now.

God is the same yesterday, today and tomorrow. He never changes, and if it is His will, I can look forward to that blessing again. So, while I continue to build my faith, I also learn to let things go. For example: I asked my mother to donate a bunch of superhero stuffed animals she found in my things while cleaning out the basement. The old me had to keep everything, and through my life I had many attachments.

While I still need to let more things go, this was a step for me in the right direction and it felt good to do it. So, it was beneficial for others, like the children who will receive a gift this year, and for myself by letting go of material things. I find it easier now to give freely, even though I considered myself a giver before all this happened.

In proverbs it clearly states, those who lend to the poor, lend to the Lord, and He will repay Him. God is telling us right here do not look for reward from man, or other people, give freely without reservation, with no expectation in return, except from God. I understand this much better now and admit it does feel good to give to others. Still, I have days where the doubt creeps in, and I wonder what will happen, as far as, how much time will I get, serve, and what my future will be like.

I am learning to take comfort in knowing that God will never leave me, nor forsake me: Hebrews 13:5. Anything I go through is a chastisement for my own good. I am being groomed to be a better man, a better example for others, and all the meantime renewing my faith. I have to accept that even when I don't see things happening, I must have faith that God is still working behind the curtains of my life, for my good, and then I have to trust in Him that He knows what He is doing. Great Faith is not achieved overnight, and I have seen His mighty work in action before.

The question that I cannot allow to take up space in my head is will He do it again? We hope for what we don't see, for how can we hope for what we do see. All scripture can be applied to our lives, with hands lifted high, hearts open, giving it completely to God, just being patient to wait and see His mighty power performed. I can and in no way will ever force anyone to believe or view things the way I do, but with my true confessions, and events that happen for me can only encourage my readers to also keep the faith!

My true confession in this chapter is this: I was ashamed to return to God, embarrassed of my failures. I doubted He would help me or forgive me. I even felt selfish asking God to help me again, until I began doing Bible studies and making a real effort to understand what I was reading. The greatest conviction for me, was when certain verses spoke to me directly, as if God Himself were whispering in my ear.

I then saw the impact some new believers were receiving from the studies I was leading as opposed to just learning from the studies I was leading as opposed to just learning from. God was now using me to help other men receive His word, and through the Holy Spirit I was able to do so. It was amazing to see people; new beginners understand what was also being revealed to me. I really have never been a fan of coincidences. I know myself, many prayers that I specifically prayed for to God and shared with no one else. When those prayers were answered, I had my confirmation. Some of us are fortunate to receive such confirmation, and even when we do not, keeping the faith is still vital to remain focused and be protected from evil things, and bad situations that happen in our lives.

Patiently I wait, and with faith, hope, and love praying that once again, God will save me, and deliver me from the pit, put me back on solid ground, and allow me to reach my full potential and purpose in life according to His will. Mark 9:23, "All things are possible to one who believes." I know with God anything is possible. I still have a long way to go, I am not out of the woods yet, but I can hope and trust in God that whatever happens, it will be for my good. Renewing my faith at rock bottom wasn't a choice, it was truly my only option!

While no one truly knows what our future holds, please keep your faith and know that someone up above is watching and working on our behalf.

CHAPTER 10

# *Puppet Master*

Most of my life I was going through the motions. Working, trying to stay above water, and enjoying my downtime with whoever I was dating at the time, or friends. I never gave thought to who I really was, and what my purpose in life was. Honestly, I wasn't making time for God, but only thanking Him when things seemed to be going well. This is all too common among people, and I was a victim of it myself.

In recent years, before my arrest I was leading a double life, kind of like being two people in one body. On one hand, I was an honest businessman, who would help anyone in need. On the other, I was a compulsive gambler, a frequent club goer, and a womanizer who thought little of other people's feelings. Let's be honest and say I was lost and selfish. Now that we have gotten that out of the way, I ask myself, who was really pulling my strings?

I was self-serving to an extent, but also serving someone else in the meantime. I was a crowd-pleaser, a people pleaser, and worse worried too often what others thought about me. At times I would tell myself I don't care what other people think about me, they don't pay my bills. My actions would show otherwise. I like so many people today used Facebook as my platform of putting my best face forward. "Hey, look at me." My life is so great.

I mean I had my business running full swing, a nice house, a newer truck, nice clothes, and I would spend money in nightclubs that most could not afford to do. My lifestyle looked glamorous to some, while in reality I was suffering inside the whole time trying to be someone I wasn't. It led me down roads of deep depression, failed relationships, and so many mistakes when it came to managing my money.

So many times, family would try to talk sense into me, but I was in control of my life, so I thought. The truth is someone was pulling my strings all along, and I was too blind, caught up in life to see it. The Devil was my puppet master. I was his MVP, most valuable player, and went out of my way to show others I was somebody! On the surface I appeared to be a successful businessman, and for a time I actually was. Again, we often show others only what we want them to see, and not the real us.

So, I would post my best self daily. I never posted the days I would lose thousands of dollars and wanted to end my life. Those days I was quiet and posted nothing. The highs and lows of the life I was living was so extreme, even I couldn't control it after a while. This is how my strings were pulled.

In 2015, when my life first began to fall apart, I would gamble to escape my failed relationship. I thought winning more money would make me happy, and it only further destroyed me. I would skip work, from the business I loved and provided for me, to go gamble. I went out two to three nights a week, dating a multitude of young women again trying to feel good about myself, and fill a void. None of these unhealthy hobbies worked for me. They only masked the real problem inside of me, and it was about to explode in my face.

I convinced myself that I had to maintain this image of success that I portrayed to everyone, and that they believed about me. I could not admit to anyone I was failing. So, I lied to myself, and I chased bad money trying to put a band-aid on wounds that were too big to cover. The story did not end well, and I was arrested in late September 2015 for a series of bank robberies that had my life in complete shambles.

The whole time, it was the Devil using my weakness against me, and fooling me in ways I could not see. After my release from prison in 2018, I thought with my renewed faith in God, and the blessing I received of being home so soon, I was ready to face life and start over.

The transition was smooth, and in no time, I picked back up with my business right where I left off and started making good money again and fast. I also had a new girlfriend who I got serious with fast, and all seemed right with the world. So, I thought.

Just three months home and my strings were being pulled again, only this time the Devil came at me from a different angle. He used a woman to distract me and destroy me. I was so in lust; I was blind to all that was happening in front of me. My newfound belief of being a loyal man convinced me that I couldn't fail as long as I was being true to someone and serving God. While I did remain faithful to this woman, she was not the right woman for me, and we were not on the same page at all. I thought I could fix her, when that wasn't my job. The devil would have me believe otherwise.

When I thought she was from God, as she often said the same about me, the truth is, The Devil put her right in front of me, knowing what I liked, and used it against me. You see, the enemy never puts something ugly in front of you, he entices you with things you think you actually want. He knew I liked beautiful women, so that's what he gave me. Never judge a book by its cover. While beautiful on the outside, the inside was just plain broken.

I was up for the challenge, not knowing it would destroy me again. When I failed to communicate with her and receive in return the emotions I gave, I became depressed. That depression led me to gambling, and the old me was back. The whole time the Devil wanted this, and he used a woman to pull my strings that would lead me to my old destructive ways. A curve ball if you will, an angle I never saw coming. What did I do? I again tried to save my image and recoup my losses so I could not only keep what I had but try to save a relationship that was failing.

I knew in my heart the money was the only thing keeping her around in the end, and that confirmed itself quickly after I was arrested again in August of 2018. Just 10 days into my jail term she left me, erased me as if I never existed. Stopped taking my calls and moved on. Deep down I never expected her to stick around, but damn, less than two weeks? After all I did for her. Still the Devil celebrated, for he accomplished his goal, and again I lost everything.

While I tried so hard to save everything and prove to the world I was somebody, I forgot to save myself. During my incarceration, with Bible studies, and lots of introspection into my life I realized this. I am somebody. I had already all the riches a man could ever want or need. I lived in a nice house, had a nice business to run and provide for myself. A family who loved me, a car, food to eat, a place to sleep comfortably, and talents to pursue in time. So, I was chasing after something I already had, but was deceived by the enemy, thinking I needed more. More to prove I was a successful person and uphold this image I believed was what made me who I was at the time.

This was a huge mistake, and my beliefs were wrong. Even though I still have great ambitions and have much to accomplish in my life, my motives will be different. I am not trying to prove to anyone that I am important, or somebody they should recognize, instead I just want to be me! In just being me, I can still make an impact in my own life, including others, and that will be successful in itself.

I have turned back to God and want Him to direct my steps, cutting the strings of the puppet master who has controlled my life for so long by using my faults and weaknesses against me. I check myself every time something happens to me or comes into my life, and I ask myself, who or where is this coming from? When it seems too good to be true, it may not be the work of God, but the Devil is once again trying to fool me by giving me instantly what I want without warning of the repercussions later. As everything that glitters is truly not gold, so are the things we get in life, that can do more harm than good in our lives.

Life happens to all of us, and sometimes so fast we lose sight of what and who really matters. This time I am using to focus on myself has revealed so much to me, and in doing so, I feel compelled to share with my readers. True stories are not just stories. They are real learning tools for us and for those around us. I look at most everything different these days, and especially what my first family means to me. When people who love us try to tell us something, it's not always to their benefit, but sometimes it's for our own good too.

I wish I listened to my mother more, surely, I would not be where I am today, telling my story from federal prison. However, I have seen the lies, the games, and the ridiculous life that I was living for what it truly was. The puppet master who was pulling my strings only to destroy me and deceive me. Two things happened last time when I got out, life and me. This time I will take a much closer look at me, before life happens again.

So, when it does, not only will I be more prepared, but with no strings attached. I have my good and bad days, we all do. We all go through hard times, suffer losses, and can be deceived by others at times. I want to make us all aware to not be deceived by the enemy by deceiving ourselves and trying to be someone we are not. I spent too much of my life trying to be the man. Now I just want to be a man. I just want to be me.

Family beach day 2018

Guys night out having fun

Mom and I at Church

My mom, an angel, Philly visit room

Still smiling

CHAPTER 11

# *All My Apologies*

When I look back on most of my regrets in life, I often wonder about the people I may have hurt, or even helped become better people for themselves. It leaves me somewhat empty, due to loss of love, time and a heart that has never fully healed. While touching on this subject, I wanted to take a chance to share some apologies with those who meant something to me at the very least. Where do I begin? Obviously, first I have made my apologies, asking for forgiveness with God.

That was most important. In doing so, I asked Him to allow me to forgive others who may have wronged me, so I can let go of that pain, and also be forgiven by Him. I will start with the most recent apology. I will apologize to the woman I most recently loved, for leaving her abruptly, and with a baby in tow. Even though there is no longer a child involved due to an unfortunate miscarriage, still I am sorry for what I put you through during that time.

I want to not further play the blame game, and mention the wrongs I endured by you, but rather use this time to say I am sorry for the things I did wrong in the relationship that could have been different. I will always have some regrets about it. Even if you do not, at this time I don't know how she feels, but can say how I feel. I am sorry I tried to change you in a short time, and wasn't more patient until you were ready to make a change for yourself. That being said, maybe someday she will forgive me, so she can let go of her resentment towards me as well.

Next, my dear mother. How truly sorry I am for letting you down again, and breaking your heart. The one woman who I always could count on, and never meant me any harm. The time I spent with you was so short, it bothers me a great deal, and hope in the future we can make up for that lost time. You are a special lady, and I am lucky to have you as a mom, please accept my apologies for all that I did wrong. Then my sister, who looked up to me, but I barely made time for. I am sorry I wasn't there more to help you as well. That will change when I come home, you can believe that.

To any women I lied to and hurt in the past, I want to take this time to apologize to you all personally. For whatever it may be worth, I am truly sorry. To my once greatest love Sarah. Wow the five years we spent together on a rollercoaster ride that ended with me going to prison, and us finally cutting ties. I know I put through some hell, and I may have apologized a million times before, but let me say again how sorry I am for any pain I ever caused you.

You were a good woman to me, and I wish I treated you better during those years together. All the gifts I gave you would not have compared to me just being faithful and loyal to you. For that, I apologize. I want to credit you for the change in me, for who I am today. I practice being a loyal man, and I was in my last relationship.

I remember telling you in prison I would be loyal to the next woman I dated, and at least I can say I was. I owe a lot of that to you. I felt your pain, when I lost you in 2015, and a year later you moved on and fell in love with someone else. I swore to myself I never wanted to cause anyone that type of pain again, simply because I know what it felt like. It is not pleasant. Then you reached out to me and tried being my friend when I came home in 2018, and I rejected you. I kind of said, "Hey, look at me now."

Using my new girlfriend as a front for happiness, and my business doing well, I only fooled myself by the mirage I used to make it seem like my life was so great. This is me being truly honest, and at the very least I hope you can see that one day. I might have been better off with your weekend visits, instead of diving into my new relationship and going through what I went through. Maybe you were looking out for me, and if so, I am sorry I didn't listen to you.

I want you to also know I am fully aware of what you did immediately after my arrest, and even still, I forgive you. That is why I won't mention it here. You see, that is what forgiveness is really all about. When you forgive a person you let it go, for good! You don't remind a person how bad they hurt you, every time there is an argument or disagreement again. True forgiveness wipes the slate clean but is so hard for many of us to do, especially when we are left with emotional scars.

This is most likely the case with my most recent ex-girlfriend. Only she came into our relationship that way already, something I cannot take credit for. Regardless, I am trying to forgive her as well, for if I hold onto the anger, and resentment it does me no good. Let's face it, she moved on, and so too must I. All my apologies to anyone I may have done wrong to or by, I never intended to intentionally hurt anyone. I was caught up in my own life, my selfish ways, and my addiction which, ultimately, consumed me all together.

As I move forward with this book, and my life, I use my mistakes to learn from them so I can be better for myself and in turn treat others better as well. That is all any of us can do after we apologize or try to make amends for what we have done wrong to anyone in our lives. I hope I didn't miss anyone, but if I did, sincerely, I forgive. I hope after all this time you may also forgive me.

# *Passion Inspired*

A fire is burning, a passion inside.
Some call it ambition, and some call it drive.

My need to make progress and be my very best.
To reach all my goals, and to call it success.

Self-motivated and driven with desire.
Filled with these flames for my drive is on fire.

A message to share, and a goal to be met.
Reaching full potential without the regret.

Plans I have made and will continue to make.
Learning from my past and all my mistakes.

Using my failures to make better decisions.
Shaping my goals doing so with precision.

Giving my best, and still giving some more.
Dreams and the visions I want to explore.

Nothing is impossible if I want to receive.
I can accomplish if I only believe.

My passion is strong and will continue to strive.
With hope for the future, all my dreams come alive.

By Michael Fanelli
Copyright 2019

# *Goals for the Future*

1. To publish my books
2. To speak publicly about addiction
3. Do volunteer work for the church
4. Rebuild my business
5. To have a family of my own
6. Become a better listener
7. Travel more
8. Donate my time to charity
9. Maintain my overall recovery
10. Make a difference in my life as well as someone else

# *Nobility Quotes*

"If I can compare myself to anything or anyone, I look at the man I was yesterday, opposite the man I am today."

"True nobility is defined only if my good intentions lead to good works."

"A noble man will make amends even with no benefit to himself, for the true benefit lies within peace knowing he did so."

"The most noble thing we can give is the gift that keeps on giving, something taught, something shared, something gained."

"While knowledge may be power, a noble man knows when and how to use it."

"Great nobility comes from experiences that humble us."

Quotes by the author: Michael Fanelli
Copyright 2019

# Hope for the Future

So much has happened to me in 39 years, I often look back analyzing it all. I tell myself that some of it had to have happened for a reason, and there are others I wish I could have avoided. No one likes to lose, especially those we love. Still, it is better to have loved and lost, than to have not ever loved anyone at all. There is hope. There's always another chance when you don't give up on yourself. This is exactly what I will never do, give up! Pain leaves us with scars, sometimes deep emotional ones, but we also learn from that pain, and we grow.

For me it is the only way, and the choice is that I am making. It is a good choice because there are few who still love me, and believe in me, and that's plenty. More importantly, I believe in myself. This is so crucial for anyone who has ever had doubts or lost hope in their lives. Believing in yourself has to be the driving factor to want to make positive changes in your life.

I have been down dark roads before and came out of them. This road I am traveling while writing this book is just another bump in the road, one that I must encounter and move on from. Still, there is hope! I look forward to re-building my small business power washing, which once was successful. I am aiming to publish not just this one, but several books that I have written, to share messages with hopes that I can make a difference in someone's life.

What a great reason to hold onto hope for, to see your work bear fruit, and sow seeds that benefit others too! It feels great to help someone, especially those around us that we love and care for. We want the very best for them, at least we should, and them the very best for us. I have many plans for the future and want God to direct my steps, blessing me along the way, so I cannot fail. Despite all of my mistakes, regrets, and failures in the past, still there is much hope! How awesome is that? It's pretty amazing if you ask me.

Don't just take my word for it, look at your life and identify all the blessings you have and may take for granted every day. Then ask yourself, is there still hope? As long as we never give up on ourselves and one another there will always be hope. A better, brighter day to look forward to, and one that I cannot wait to see. To fulfill my purpose, and help others discover their meaning in life if I have the opportunity to do so. Keep the hope alive! No matter what has happened to us, who has hurt us, left us or forgotten about us, never forget who you are, and believe that there is hope for the future.

-A letter from the author: Michael Fanelli

CHAPTER 12

# *Living For The People*

Living for the people I was more concerned about showing others I was somebody who mattered, was important, and successful. If I was living for myself, none of that would have mattered to me at all. For the fear of judgement or rejection could not have affected who I was. That being said, if I was okay with me, and content with who I was. Due to my actions that have led me back to where I am, in prison, I see now that I was living for the people, and especially in my relationship by catering to her needs before my own.

There is nothing wrong with wanting to lead by example, or inspire other people, as long as it doesn't destroy you in the process. Some people are okay with who they are in life, even if they don't have their lives together by society's standard. That means they either don't care what other people think, or deny their own faults and do nothing to change their situation for the better. When it came to me making positive changes for myself, I looked for that commendation from others, instead of being humble and being content with who had begun the change in me.

It should have been all about God, but I wanted my will done, by His grace. Reality is, God just doesn't work that way. I was still a baby Christian, still learning and not ready yet to face the real me. I knew scripture, I quoted, it, and I could take you anywhere in the

Bible to show you it, but I wasn't fully receiving it. Again, knowing the truth, and living the truth, are two completely different things. My work is not finished. I know God will continue to work on me, and I will mature in my spiritual life. When I do, I will live for myself, and not be living for the people, or looking for their opinions to validate who I am.

A lot of us get caught up living for others, in a misplaced belief about who we are, or our purpose is in life if you want to truly live for others in a healthy way, you have to be happy and healthy for you first! Very simply put, I can relate my actions to scripture located in Ecclesiastes, known as The Preacher. The story of King Solomon who was considered the wisest man who ever lived, and the richest kind to ever rule. Here's how: He spoke of an evil under the sun that he saw.

A person who was blessed to earn great wealth toil hard, yet not be able to enjoy it for himself. Only to be left for someone else to enjoy. The story of my life! For years I worked hard only to gamble and give it all away.

When I did spend some of it, it was usually on others. Buying lavish gifts for women I dated or treating others to nights out when I frequented nightclubs. How little I did for myself, and in the end, was able to enjoy! I receive the scripture now for what it is. Why work so hard just to give it away? Now sharing a fortune is not a bad thing, it is not what I'm saying. Not being able to enjoy any of it yourself is evil. Looking back at what I could have had, or done, or to places I could have traveled could only lead me to self-resentment.

Self-resentment will tear you down! I know it firsthand. So, while I'm renewing my faith, and rewiring my mind, I will have to see next time who I live for. My actions will reveal themselves. It's nice to have followers and fans. A cheering section can make you feel great. Still, I have to be my number one fan so I can be complete, and happy with who I am, no matter what. This is all the difference between those who are truly okay, and those who just believe that they are okay, they are the ones who will make a real effort to change. This is all the difference when you're just living for you and living for the people.

I'll give an example: if a person in their 40's or so are still living home with mom and dad it's okay for a short while. Now if they have been for years, have their own children there as well, do not work full time, don't have a car, and they are doing little to nothing about it to change, then they are just okay with their situation, due to familiarity. I call this just plain lazy.

If this is someone's idea of okay, I would rather live for the people, but it's not okay, so change is required. We all fear change, when we should embrace it. When we finally accept who we are after positive changes improve our lives, now automatically the people we once looked to perform for will notice us anyway. Working on yourself is not only beneficial to you, but for you. It can in turn benefit others as well, serving a greater purpose than we had originally intended it to. This hit me like a truck and opened my eyes to who I really was living for, when all the time I was not allowing God to finish what He started in me.

Today I embrace His intervention and can be excited about my future for my good, by his will and not mine. Let's all live for ourselves and not get lost living for the people, especially so many who won't care about us once we are gone.

When I walked through the door, I left my troubles of the world outside, for she made my house feel like a home. The great quality of a good woman. I felt not only understood and appreciated, but I felt whole and complete. This is a stretch even for me, and I hope someday I can tell this person thank you for that feeling of immense love that she showed me at that time. I was neither lonely, nor alone. You can feel lonely around family, even friends, but there is no greater feeling of loneliness than feeling lonely around your spouse or significant other.

This can make you feel empty, and more alone than you've ever felt before. So, when considering if you ever feel alone, look at your surroundings and also to the person who is next to you. Then ask yourself, how do you feel? If you feel lonely, that must be addressed with that person, otherwise get used to being alone even if they are present with you. Some people don't even realize this is happening until it's too late, or familiarity sets in. It dooms many relationships, and no one should be lonely in life with those they love, or be left out in the cold feeling empty, and alone.

A common saying is, "If you are lonely, get a dog." Maybe we are better off. Still, I think deep down inside of us all, nobody wants to be alone. Also, it does not feel good to be lonely. I hope this letter from the author has shed some light on the subject, and helps us all to be better understood and able to better understand our partners, and to be able to be noticed in all of our relationships in a healthy way.

By: Michael Fanelli

# A Letter from the Author
## Lonely or Alone?

Have you ever been in a crowded room full of people and still felt all alone? How about with just one person in a small room, yet feel so lonely? Ask yourself what's worse? Me personally, there is nothing like feeling lonely in a relationship, while the person is lying or sitting right next to you. Have you ever experienced this feeling? The difference is you cannot be alone, but still feel lonely with someone. This was a problem in one of my relationships that eventually failed.

We all want to be noticed, accepted, thought of, and loved. What about being fully known? Can any of us know our partner or have them know us this well? A lot of questions here I know but think about it and soon enough you will know what I'm talking about. I can be in a room full of people and not feel lonely. To be at home with a person you love and feel like they are not there, well it doesn't get any lonelier than that, even if they weren't there at all.

How can this be? While the person may physically be in your company, we feel lonely or alone because their mind and heart are someplace else. I experienced this feeling with someone I loved. When we were both just feet away from each other, or were even in two different rooms in the house, I felt lonely at times. I would try to convince myself things were good, and I was happy just because she was there.

Tell me, what good is a body without a mind paying any attention? This is why after years I've discovered that looks fade, and physical attractions only last so long. What stands the true test of time is compatibility. The ability to love one another for who they are and be stimulated by them mentally more than just physically. At the end of the day, can two people get along well together, and look forward to each other's company.

I also once experienced that feeling, and it was the opposite of feeling alone. It feels priceless! To come home from work and your spouse makes you feel welcomed, missed, loved, and appreciated, and understands you and your needs. If you can find this in a life partner stick with that person. These are the big traits and they are important. This one-woman in particular would not only cook for me, or help me around the house, but something far greater than the two.

CHAPTER 13

# *See Me Through My Eyes*

I had to meet myself, in order to change myself. When I say this, I had to see myself in someone else, and not like who I see. All of my life I was seeing things through my own eyes. Of course, it was my world, and everyone and everything was my oyster. It began when I was a kid. I was spoiled by my parents, mainly by my father. When I was punished for a bad thing, I cried about it, and soon after the punishment was lifted. This behavior continued all through to my teenage years, even into my twenties. When I couldn't get my way with family, I would stomp my feet like a child, and get my way.

It is where my manipulation began. Seeing that this worked, why stop it there? Over the years, I talked myself and my way out of so many situations, or undesirable things, I was becoming a real pro at it. This behavior would follow me into personal relationships, where I would lie to and manipulate my partners, and ultimately get my way. It didn't always work with every female, but it worked so often I continued to see things my way, and why not? In my late 30's when I met someone like me, that all changed.

Let's just say the manipulator would become the manipulated. This person was headstrong like me, and set in her ways, and also very used to getting her way. At first, we seemed to be a good match for each other, until conflict began and she didn't want to see things from my perspective, or through my eyes. Slowly but surely, I was starting to see a person I did not like or want to face. I saw a mirror image of me! Now we were not the same in all ways, definitely not, but she could manipulate me with her smile, let alone words.

The sad truth here was I wasn't trying to manipulate or get over on somebody for the first time in my life, but it was now happening to me. Payback is a bitch! Karma had definitely caught up to me, and it destroyed me. For so long I have been expecting others to see me through my own eyes and didn't care much about how they felt. That evil had repaid me, and it took for that to happen for it to make a change in me. My whole perspective on life is different now, and this was one contributing factor.

I don't like the person I saw, nor the person I was. How could I be that person for so long? In relationships we tend to say, "Well, I guess you met your match." For me, I was out matched, used, lied to, and manipulated by her. She used my own emotions against me. This is truly how the devil works. Nothing hurts more than being used by someone you love.

Even when we make mistakes, or tell little lies, being faithful with a pure heart leaves you open to this type of hurt. I finally was able to see myself for who I really was. Today I'm glad not to be that person any longer. My family's feelings matter to me. My significant other's will also matter to me just as much as my own feelings do. So many people bulldoze in relationships. Usually one person over the other, and that one party usually knows they have control over the situation, and control over the other person's feelings.

This is wrong, manipulative, and evil. Both people matter equally, and I saw enough red flags in one relationship to last me a lifetime. Getting a taste of your own medicine never feels good, but it can do you some good, when you recognize it for what it really is. I'm bearing a big truth here. I manipulated people for years, with looks, personality, charm and emotions. This is me being true and honest. Not everyone will admit who they are, or once were. For me, it's just another demon to bury, so I can live a better, happier, more meaningful life.

I lost all those that I once truly loved, so being honest, I have nothing more to lose. I have no intentions to ever try to get over on anyone again, so this feels good to come clean. Some people may not look at me the same way ever again, and that's okay. It's always a chance you take when you are honest with people. It's also better than taking more chances to see things one way and trying to manipulate others.

I don't want that karma, and none of us should. While some may never meet themselves, whether through reflections of other people, or through their own eyes, be sure that you will catch up to you regardless. When your ways are malicious or not with good intentions. So, can you see me through my eyes? Do you see anyone else? I see a new me, and honest me, a better me, and I'm actually starting to like this guy.

We can all appreciate the truth, when the fog is lifted from our eyes, and we see things from a true and clear perspective. With respect for ourselves, and others. I'm glad I was able to show you what took me so long to see, to see me through my eyes.

I have left out the names of some not to publicly bash their character as mine was one done. Though my stories are true, and some may recognize themselves in them, that wasn't the message I intended. I used the true stories to show who I was, and how I saw things, naturally from my eyes of course, and my point of view. I truly hope that this chapter, among them all my readers and the people who support me as well can really see the truth in all of this.

To learn from it, and apply it to their own lives, as I am beginning to do. We see so much in our lifetime through these delicate eyes we have, we can easily become accustom to certain beliefs, and views. We then do not like to be challenged on them, because we feel like it is a personal attack on us. While it feels personal, it really is not. It is just the way we are used to living and how we have become programmed from an early age. This is learned behavior, and with personal experience it is so hard to change.

Especially since our beliefs have been the same for years and we live by them. We don't always look at things this way, but when we do, it becomes clear that we are essentially biased by our own beliefs. Therefore, we gave little attention or thought to others and their beliefs, especially when ours are attacked or challenged. I hope that makes sense to you, since I tried to make it simple enough to understand.

I was compelled to write this book for many reasons. It changed along the way, but one thing remained constant, the truth. These are my true confessions, and myself fully exposed bearing all my truth. Seeing life only through my eyes has done more damage than good and narrowed my whole perspective on life. Today being honest, and open minded has broadened that horizon in great lengths, and with unlimited possibilities for the future.

Being honest may have some downfalls, but it sure has greater benefits. You can be the judge of you. Try applying your own truth through others' eyes and ask yourself what you see. If you see fog, then your view may be one way, or narrow. If you see clear, then you not only can know your truth, but live it as well. I am grateful to see things in a new healthier way. Now applying these new views and principles is all that is left to do!

Let your eyes see the truth, share the truth and hep you live your truth. What a pair of beautiful eyes you have gained in this process.

CHAPTER 14

# *The Lost Chronicles*

As I look back on my life, the past 39 years have had many ups and downs. There has been more loss than achieved, and it brings me to this chapter. I can honestly say I have loved deeply at least three times. All three have been lost, and that makes me three for three in failed relationships. I have been engaged twice and should have married twice. I could have been a father three times as well. I often think how different my life would have been, had I become a father.

I believe it would have changed me, for the better and made a huge impact in my life. Giving me a real sense of responsibility, other than myself, which was all I was ever used to. My twenties were mostly spent partying, dating, and being wild, doing whatever my heart desired. While I had a lot of fun, and have a lot of memories, still I have a lot of regrets. I have very little to show for in my life other than those memories. Many of my friends would often say I had a great life, but I see a meaningless one compared to those who had made their own families and had children of their own.

They would come home to a house full of love and feel complete. While for years my bed may have been filled with various women, I remained empty inside as far as I can remember. One night of fun, the next a day of emptiness, chasing that night before every weekend that followed. I can't say I miss those days much, and wish I made better choices back then. Today, being back in prison, I watch the world live without me yet again, and old memories creep in.

I think what if I did this, or was faithful to this person, how things could have been so different. I know dwelling on the past will not bring me any progress in the future, but I will not allow those same mistakes to happen if it's in my control. When I came home in 2018, my longest love had reached out to me, and I had a chance to reconcile with her. Only now I was in love with someone else, and I kind of used that moment to gloat and say, "Look at me now." It's backfired on me, and now I wonder what if I walked down memory lane and tried starting over with the old flame?

I may never know. Three years had passed since our relationship ended, and our lives had changed a lot, but not so much. And obviously she still had some feelings there, enough anyway to contact me again after three years. Maybe she wanted to sabotage my new relationship—seeing I was happy and didn't want that for me. I will never know for sure, and I guess now it doesn't really matter anyway.

I can only imagine at least another three years will go by before I am released, and that's being hopeful. At that point, six years will have passed between our lives, and the chances then of us ever getting back together are very slim if not none. I know she wants a family, as did I, but time is no longer on my side, for I am temporarily gone from the free world that people live in every day. This is just one of my lost chronicles. One of many to list. Approaching 40 years old, another window is closing on me, my chances of ever becoming an actor or speaker on television.

I always wanted to act, and I spent years doing amateur auditions, and I even used my charisma in my business—power washing—all the time. Also, at my birthday parties where I used to dress up like Batman, Spiderman or Superman and entertain kids for various events. I enjoyed that so much and made some decent money doing it too. For me, it was more than just money, it was a chance to perform and show off my acting skills. I began this type of entertainment at age 24 and continued doing it until I was 36 years old, up until my last arrest in 2015.

When I was released in early 2018, I returned to power washing and would often post entertaining videos at work, but never got back into child entertainment. I hope to do so again someday, if I am young enough to do so. I wonder if time will be on my side. I was blessed with so many gifts, and talents that I am often haunted by my choices that lead me here to prison. I know I never reached my full potential in life, and with my gift of expression, in my writing, I hope to do so, and not have another regret to write about, adding to my lost chronicles.

Regrets are like parasites that eat away at your brain, until you become exhausted or can't take it anymore. Life here on Earth is limited, and we are not promised tomorrow. We have to make the most of who we are and what we have, or our regrets, missed opportunities, and even failures will become like lost pages in our lives, so-called "lost chronicles." Knowing what I know now, man, I wish I could rewind back to when I was 25 years old and restart my life then, with both businesses running. I'd manage my money a whole different way and make better choices.

Too bad I don't have a time machine, the only time machine that exists is in our head, our memories. All we can do from here is make changes, and that's all I can do. These lost chronicles are like scattered memories all over the place, taking me from one time to another in my life, and with pain along the way. Time waits for no one, and also stops for no one. Time is so precious and we all at times have taken it for granted.

While the world continues to live without me, I am trying my best to use this down time again to reshape myself from the inside out. I want to reprogram my mind while my heart heals from the losses I endured. I sincerely hope that future chronicles in my life will be pages of happiness, inspired by hope, determination, and hard work that wasn't wasted. The saddest thing in life is wasted talent. Our gifts were meant to be used to the fullest, to benefit ourselves and others. As I step into the 2nd half of my life, I have plenty of guides, mistakes to look back on.

These guides can now be guidelines on how to live a better, healthier, and more meaningful life. That is really all our past is, memories we can cherish and learn from. Either way, the past can be used greatly to teach us how to live in the here and now. We all have lost chronicles, pages in our lives that we look back on and wonder what if I had done this or that, and how different my life could have been.

Still, we can make changes and start living for today, and for ourselves, doing the things we want to do with the resources available to us. A big regret for me was that I had the finances to do a lot of things I didn't get a chance to do last time. I wanted to travel more and go skydiving. I took for granted this time, thinking there is always tomorrow. Some people never get a chance to do all they want in life, because they cannot afford to do it financially.

That was not my problem, but still I failed to do so much, and accomplish what I set out to do. When we start to live life doing what we want, at least we are moving forward with hope and happiness making better memories and less regrets. I hang on today with hope that I again will be blessed with the opportunity to achieve my goals, and enjoy my life doing the things I want to do and share those experiences with someone special. I have enough lost chronicles to last me a lifetime.

It is time to start living for me, and for anyone who can relate to this, start living for yourself! Every day is a new day. A second chance to rewrite our script, but time is limited. Time cannot be taken for granted. It must be utilized efficiently, and healthy, so we can achieve real meaning in our lives, and have happy memories to look back on. Our lives will also be examples for our children, our loved ones, and those closest to us. I hope that the next chronicles, or pages of my life will be me fulfilling my dreams, my purpose, and accomplishing all that I set out to do, while enjoying my days that are given under the sun.

While in county jail, I wrote this letter in an emotional state, never expecting an answer in return. People said I was crazy and wasting my time. Here is that response. A reply from the President of the United States, Mr. Donald. J. Trump.

## THE WHITE HOUSE
### WASHINGTON

November 26, 2018

Dear Mr. Fanelli,

Thank you for taking the time to write and share your story with President Donald J. Trump. He is honored by the opportunity to serve you and the American people.

White House staff reviewed your correspondence and forwarded it to the appropriate Federal agency for further action. For additional information about the Federal government in the meantime, please visit www.USA.gov or call 1-800-FED-INFO.

Respectfully,

The Office of Presidential Correspondence

So maybe I am not so crazy after all? Even so, I can say I wrote the president and the White House responded! I just thought I would share this amazing event and show my readers that truly anything is possible in life!

CHAPTER 15

# *Money & Happiness*

Most of us spend our entire lives looking for some type of completion. We look for things, or someone to complete us. In essence, we are all searching for happiness. To find what I call a little place of happiness, I have narrowed down two subjects, one goal. This chapter is one of my true confessions, in which I believe many of you will be able to relate to. The world has a lot to offer from an earthly perspective. We all went to do well and provide for our families and ourselves. We want to get our little piece of the pie in life, and to be happy while doing it. Then we want to share that happiness with someone meaningful to us.

While there is nothing wrong with that, consider this: does money really make us happy? Of course, we need it to live. Money is not a bad or good thing. It has no morals. It is a tool, and is only defined by how it is used, depending on whose hands it is in. Money can get you a whole lot of material possessions. It can provide us with a sense of security. It also can buy us comfort. One thing that money cannot buy is happiness. Now some of you may say, 'Hey, if I won the lottery, I would be extremely happy' At first maybe, but then money does something else too, it changes us.

It becomes more about who we are, and we make the common mistake of letting it define us. I made this very mistake and so often, I had misplaced belief that if I had enough money, I would be happy. How wrong I was. There was a time I had acquired plenty of what money can bring. We are never satisfied with how much we have, and always find ourselves wanting more. A proven statistic in America is that if the average American can pay their bills and have a little bit extra to do what they want to do in life, they are happy. This is based on an income of $65,000 or more, This is just enough to provide for a family and meet their basic needs.

I can tell you I made more than that, with no family of my own to support, and still wasn't happy. This is because happiness doesn't come from stuff, it comes from within. The human race has been programmed over time to believe that the more we acquire, the happier we will be. This is false, and more harmful to us than good. I am not saying in anyway that money cannot do a lot for us, I am just saying it shouldn't dictate who we are and our principles for standard living. Although it does for so many, and you guessed it, I fell into the money trap as well.

While it feels great to be able to buy gifts for ourselves and others, will it bring us true happiness? Not everyone will agree with me, but I am sure many will understand the view I am portraying here. So, we must separate the two. Money is a tool, needed to pay our bills, and help us survive in this life. Happiness is something we can feel, and obtain for free, and should not be based on how much money we have or acquire over our lifetime.

Finding a good partner to share our lives with is a priceless gift, and one that money surely cannot buy. Accomplishing a deep inspired goal starts off with a vision we have inside, and again something that money cannot buy us. Money can only magnify who we are already. If we are good people, then it's safe to assume we will be good people with money. If we are bad people, then we might in turn be bad people with money. However, the case may be, we should not allow money to change us, and make us who we are.

I chased after bad money time and time again. I had a sick belief that money defined me, and if I had enough money, I was successful. We can do great things with money, I was successful. We can do great things with money, or it can destroy us. Sadly, I let it destroy me, and therefore cannot ever look at money the same way again. This will not happen to all of us, but for those who have been blinded by it, please know that money is just a tool we use, and we should not be used by it. Unfortunately, many of us have been and will continue to, and never truly find that happiness we are all searching for.

So that takes care of money. So, what about this mysterious happiness we are all searching for? We all want to be loved, noticed, and appreciated for who we are, will this make us happy? For some, maybe, but how about looking at happiness from a new perspective. Ask yourself during your busy lives of working, raising children, and social friendships are you at peace? Do you know you have to be at peace to truly be happy? Monks have discovered this theory long ago, and some of the poorest people in American claim to be happy.

How can that be? Sound strange to any of you. It sure did to me. It did before because my standard that I was judging happiness on was based on money. If you had it, you were happy, if you didn't well you weren't. This was a false assumption, and one that I learned the hard way.

I look back and realize that some of the happiest times of my life were me just being next to the person I loved, in the house, without spending a dollar! Sure, we had money to pay the rent, and buy groceries, the basic stuff we need to live and survive. We just didn't care about money to the point of it being needed for us to have fun and enjoy life with each other's company. This is why I said earlier finding a good, loving, faithful partner is priceless.

Even then, we should not base our happiness on them, but then can only add to the happiness we already have in our self. It's really simple when you think about it, however many of us will never truly find it, and be fooled at what it means to be truly happy. Happiness is not something you can buy. It is not a prize at the end of a magical journey. Happiness is a state of being and it all begins with us. We have to truly love our self-first, and be okay with who we are, if we are ever going to experience true happiness.

Are we ready to do that? I sure am, after years that I lost chasing a false sense of security, and after a happiness I could just never seem to catch, I finally realized it was time to slow down, stop running and learn to be content with that I have already. I lost a lot chasing happiness, only because I was running the wrong race. Imagine spending your whole life walking in the wrong direction and for nothing in return but hurt, regret, and pain to look back on.

The true definition of insanity: doing the same thing over and over and expecting a different result. For years, that was the story of my life. If I have money, I will be happy, over and over again. I have almost nothing today, as I write this book, well, except a family who loves me, food to eat, clothes on my back, a sound mind, a better heart and outlook on life. Finally, and not to be under stated, I have the one who provided me with it all. I have God, who loves me. I am the richest I have ever been and can appreciate all that I have in life now, because I learned to separate the two things, we search for the most money and happiness!

I look forward to a new happiness that I can live and share with others in my life. I am starting now, even while here in prison, and can only do more once I am free again to appreciate all the beauty this world has to offer, without letting it define who I am. We all want a little piece of happiness. It can be achieved when you search deep inside of yourself and see who you are, and ask yourself am I truly happy? If at that moment your heart is filled with warmth and you can't help but smile, I think you made have ended that exhausting search, and you found the most priceless gift we cannot buy, the gift of happiness!

CHAPTER 16

# *Giving Up Control*

As human beings, and for me as well, I believe one of the hardest things to do in our lives is to give up control. I am not talking about controlling others, but control over our own lives to the point that we do not become reckless or hurt ourselves or others while doing so. I am talking about control over things that sometimes we have no control over, and letting it play it out however the cards may fall. This was super hard for me to do, especially since I believed most of my life that I was in control of things, and the final author of my life.

I was mistaken in so many ways and began to realize that I had to give up control and let some things go. To whom was I going to trust my life with, after all, who could possibly care more about me, than myself? This is where I turned the page in my life and gave thought to giving my cares back to God. I wasn't used to this, and for me I felt afraid and unsure to say the least. I by now, was so used to doing things my way, that I was completely out of my element, and anticipation of the unknown would begin to become the devil's playground in my head.

It kept me up at night, it affected my appetite, and also affected my behavior towards other people, and myself. I wanted this to change, and so I prayed to God to help me let go, and give Him control over my life, and let Him be the final author of my outcome, while pending sentencing on my second federal term. This was scary, and made me uneasy, but then I thought, what real control did I really have? Sure, I could write letters and apologize for my mistakes, but that could do only so much. For ultimately, if it was in God's plan for me to prevail and be victorious at accomplishing any goal, then He would allow it and nothing I could do would change that.

I look back on my life and see how little control I really had over most situations. Sure, I was blessed by achieving some success in my small local business. Was it me? Or was it God just allowing the gift that He gave me to bear fruit? Things went so smooth that today I believe it was all God. I merely was a vessel just carrying out His will for my life.

I was blessed with family who cared for me and loved me. I was blessed with a good business, and I was given all that I could possibly need to survive, be successful, and make it in the fallen world that we live in today. One thing was missing. I still wasn't happy. Today I believe part of that void was me always trying to control every situation in my life, whether it would be work, relationships, and anything I saw fit that went according to my plans. All of those plans eventually failed.

They failed because I had no real control, only the illusion of one. That illusion came from me mostly getting my way, and thinking was the author of it. I was wrong, and that belief has cost me so much. It has not cost me the one thing I could never lose, or not return to, I still have God. It was Him all along blessing me, and allowing the gifts in my life, I just wasn't acknowledging Him or His work. Even in prison as I surrounded myself again with Christian me, I allow them to speak more than I do, and this also is me being out of my element.

Hence the term God gave us two ears and one mouth, it was time for me to start listening and accepting who was in control of my life. This stage was and will not be easy for anyone. It surely wasn't easy for me, and believe me, I still have my days. Only now I am making a conscious effort through prayer and action to ask God to do His will in my life, and then let go, and just trust Him to do just that. If I interfere, then I am not trusting, if I am not trusting God, then I am not believing. If I don't believe, then I am not practicing real faith.

So how does a person who has been making decisions for them-selves like me, for their whole adult life, wrong or right, just simply give up that much control? Good question, and my answer is this. Look at your whole life and ask yourself this: are you happy? Do you have peace? Have all your goals been accomplished? If not, then ask yourself why not? Ask yourself who is really in control? Success financially is a great thing, but it won't necessarily mean your life is in complete control. There are many wealthy people who are still very unhappy and satisfied with their lives. Tell this to a poor person, and they would say I would be happy a rich man's money, and some would believe it would solve most if not all of their problems. On the surface maybe, but inside not possible. Simply because all the money in the world cannot guarantee you that tomorrow is prom-ised. No one has that much control over life, and only one person truly knows our fate, our destiny, our beginning and our end. The benefit of completely letting go is the relief allowed by worrying less, if not worrying at all, and that is the point of giving up control I am talking about.

It is not only less stressful, but healthier for us in so many ways, but for years I was blind to this, and I expect a lot of my readers will still not understand how to do so. We are born creatures of habit, and like some habits, we tend to have a bad habit of worrying about everything, which prompts us to plan ahead, and essentially control things in our life. Planning ahead is a good thing, and I encour-age anyone to prepare for life, but no matter how much we prepare, things can change in an instant, and we can find out then how little control we really have in the big scheme of things. Life happens to us, and around us, no matter how much we maneuver around it.

This is why giving up control can be beneficial, because trusting God—who knows us better than anyone, and who is fully capable of taking care of us—is the much better choice for our life then the simple planner that we know every day in ourselves. No one is per-fect, no matter how hard we try to be. We try, we fail, and we try again. This is normal. For me, it was time to try things His way, and see that His plan for my life was better than my own. I still have my days, and by no means was it easy to do, but it has helped me see life from a whole new perspective, and I hope my readers can experience this same discovery as I have.

It was long overdue for me to let go. Not just material things, things that have little meaning in life, but let go with my heart, the purest thing in my body to freely give up. This was me allowing God inside to work on me, and now through me to do His will, and direct my steps according to His plan. I am far from the finish line, and cannot see the road ahead as clear as I would like to, but I am trusting and hoping that the road I am on, is finally the right one.

In closing on this subject, giving up control doesn't mean that you should wander aimlessly, just because we love God, and trust you Him in our care. It means stepping back sometimes and looking at certain situations and coming to depend on God more. There is nothing too great, or impossible for God. We can hope that His blessings will align with our own plans, but must believe whatever His plan is, it is for our good and his good purpose as well. We don't always like what is good for us, and we definitely are hesitant to change.

Change brings about fear, but the good news is it also it brings about hope! Hope for a better life. A better plan. A better example we can share and leave with others to follow. Change will begin when we let go of things we cannot control, or try to control. Change will not always be easy, but it can be exciting. Just like watching a movie you have never seen before, like that movie plot, so does your life have twists, and turns. Allow God to smooth out those rough turns in your life, and bring about a change within you, one that can benefit you, and everyone you come into contact with.

That is the power of letting go and giving up control! We can all look forward to an uncertain future, even as we plan for what we might want, or thing is best for us. Be mindful that when road bumps or speed traps come, it may be a sign for you to give up, let go, and allow God to work in your life. This happened for me, and I hope it will continue to do so in a healthy, positive way, leading me to a more productive, meaningful, fulfilling, but more importantly a happier and peaceful life! The more we let go, the more we can expect to receive.

CHAPTER 17

# *Daily Life In Jail*

Being incarcerated is something you never want to experience and for many reasons. The obvious ones are being away from your family, or loved ones, losing all you have worked for, and just about anything that comes with your freedom. The one other important thing that most people overlook is what we will do with our time? I swore when I was released the first time, I would never again say I was bored outside. The world is at your fingertips. To name a few things: unlimited television programs, internet access, freedom to travel anywhere at any time, eating good food, sleeping in a comfortable bed, and enjoying peace and quiet in your own home when you should choose to do so, this is a priceless one.

All of these privileges are taken away in jail, so I would like to mention what most of the inmate population does, and what I do as well. Weekdays and weekends are pretty much the same. The average guy in jail will usually watch sports, Jerry Springer, play cards, play basketball, play chess, or sit in the day room and tell war stories about their past lives, at high volumes, and at times yelling where anyone on the unit can heart them. I call this frivolous talk, or cheap talk. A common practice in jail. Also, there are others getting high on drugs like K2, a synthetic form of marijuana that gives you an out of body experience and can be dangerous and deadly.

Have you noticed that these select ones are the winners I am talking about? Not quite. Then you have the other type of inmate, the quiet type who reads mostly and stays to themselves. I fall in between and here's how. On a normal day I watch the news around 12pm after I do some typing or reading. After dinner I usually draw and get into some creative artwork and make cards for other inmates. I call this productive and constructive time. I stay away from large foolish crowds of people who look for trouble or cheap entertainment.

I enjoy working on art, or writing material, and I get paid to do so sometimes. It is all beneficial all the way around and how I usually spend most of my time. I also make time daily for my Bible reading. My prayers to God, and my reflection of all my past mistakes. I drink a lot of coffee, it's like my jailhouse addiction. Especially on weekends when I sleep in till 11am or so. I wake up and immediately make a cup of instant coffee, a far cry from my usual cup of Starbucks when I am home. I would like to name other hobbies, but unfortunately that is pretty much it. There is so little to do here, but think, and try to work on yourself, or you can learn to be a better criminal like a lot of others try doing. It is a sad environment, and one you can count yourself lucky to never experience.

My gift of writing and artwork do serve me a great purpose in jail, because often other men seek me out for small projects or things they need done. Holidays are the busiest time, especially Christmas, or Valentine's Day. Almost everyone wants to send their significant other a card. I incorporate a poem sometimes to go with the occasion and can get an extra dollar for that. So, I will give you a breakdown on how many values has decreased as a man when compared to outside of jail vs. inside.

Clearly, you cannot compare the two, especially because I previously owned and operated my own business and didn't work on an hourly rate. But if the two were compared, here are the facts. Outside I would average $75 to $100 power washing. In jail, I charge an average of $3 a card. In which I spend three hours making it front to back. That's just $1 an hour, a huge 99% decrease from my outside business. So why do I do it? Clearly not for the money, even though the extra few dollars help here and there. I do it to pass the time, stay out of trouble, and as always I enjoy helping others and bringing a smile to someone's face.

It is really amazing when you see your talents done for so little, it makes you truly appreciate what you have outside in the free world. No matter how you try to pass the time in here, it crawls compared to the free world. Minutes feel like hours, days like weeks and months like years. Nothing compares to the simple freedoms we have at home.

One other healthy hobby or habit you can adopt in here is working out. A common practice among most of us. I would like to say for the most part, free from the drugs and alcohol in the outside world, smaller portion diets, and more time to exercise. With this combination you could get into really good shape fast if you are dedicated. On my last federal bid, after coming out of a wheelchair, due to an injury to my right leg and surgery that followed. I gained over 40 pounds and became out of shape.

I began working out, and during the last four to five months before my release I lost it all and seven pounds more. I left in great shape and was ready to work again fit as I could be. I haven't started that training again yet, but I will on the downslope of my sentence. Daily life in jail is frustrating because you are surrounded with people you don't like or would normally associate with outside. It's noisy most of the time, people can be selfish, rude and plain disrespectful. There are lines for the email computer, the phone, just about everything that people cherish in here.

I tend to separate myself from that. I write letters mostly, call me old fashioned, but it works, it builds patience and it keeps me out of those long lines. In prison, I would often go to the yard when it's freezing cold, knowing most inmates would be staying inside. I find this to be a time of peace. Finding what I call peace among chaos is very rare to come by in jail or prison. So, you see there are many reasons to stay free and obey the law, and yet so many of us take those freedoms and privileges for granted. Freedom is so precious!

Some days, I wake up in here and feel lost. I am disgusted with my past mistakes and choices, yet somewhat helpless other than the fact I have to deal with them day to day. Waiting once again for the glorious day I can be free to live and fully enjoy my life again with a better appreciation and a greater meaning and purpose for my life.

Until that day, this is what life is like, a Groundhog Day of madness, and wasted time overall despite the lessons we can learn from them.

I have asked myself 1,000 times, why did you have to lose all you had again to realize how good you had it? A question that can torment or haunt anyone. The greatest fear of being in pre-trial incarceration is not knowing how much time you are going to get, and ultimately not knowing when you are going to go home and be free. That is a scary part of no control over your life in that aspect. Still, I try to utilize the time I have in a positive, productive, and constructive way. Something I can learn this time that I didn't or should have learned last time.

I guess you could say I am somewhat useful or important, even in here, but I would pass any day for a taste of freedom and the chance to accomplish all of my goals that I am setting out to achieve. What I began in here last time, I will let my gifts work for me, and not against me. I won't forget what daily life in jail was like, like I did so soon last time. It will be a strong reminder to keep me on track and guide me as well.

Jail is no place to live your life, it can be avoided though the experience is priceless. I call it my college education and my tuition is my freedom. Blood, sweat, and tears. A very heavy price to pay. My message at the end of all this is clear, obey the law, cherish your loved ones, and pursue all of your dreams and goals in life. Life is too short as it is, to waste time, especially time away from those you love, and time away from what you could be doing as a free person outside. The road ahead will be challenging, highs, lows, and plenty of frustrations and sad days, all part of being in jail. One thing for sure, my outlook has changed dramatically, and my focus is on what really matters, and those who matter as well. Time is so precious, as I will, we all must use it wisely!

# CHAPTER 18

# Lessons That I've Learned

On February 20th, 2019 I found myself looking out the window of the jail law library and watching the snow fall. Not only wishing I was outside to enjoy the snow, but to be free in it. One week from this day the 27th would be exactly one year to the day I was set free and released from prison. Needless to say, a painful moment to remember while once again sitting in jail facing more years to come before I will be set free again. This day, like many others, I think about all the hard lessons that I had to learn, and experience once again.

To name some prominent ones, I can begin by saying that I learned to never put a woman I barely know before God, and my family again. This was a huge mistake. I neglected those who truly loved me, and had proven so over time, for someone I fell in love with, who in return did not love me back in the same manner. When I got arrested and lost everything, who was there? Family. Where was she? Gone and in record time. A lesson that haunts me to this very day. I have also learned not to put my full trust in people, a sure disappointment when I did almost every single time.

Expectations of others can be a one-way trip down a road I call disappointment lane. I traveled that road or years and ended up right back where I started, disappointed and alone, with many regrets. I am not saying that you cannot trust anyone but be careful with whom you do. Trust is a key component in any form of relationship, and one I found in very few people I have known throughout my life. Another lesson that I am learning, and is a big one, is to be patient. Easier said than done, for someone like me who was used to getting things done, multi-tasking, and basically used to getting his way.

Patience, because my impulsive behavior was the driving force behind all my poor choices and bad decisions. I was usually in a hurry, and it hurt me more times than none. The time needed to think and weigh out my options was not done rationally, and with patience. A hard lesson that has ultimately cost me my freedom, basically everything.

I learned not to care so much what other people think about me, especially those not close to me, and on-lookers on social media. What was I trying to prove to people who really did not care about me, and only enjoyed the entertainment I provided, or any drama about my life? Behind closed doors nobody really cares, and you are long forgotten once you are gone and yesterday's news. I learned this twice, the hard way.

I am again learning to value my life for what it was and working on being content with all that I had or have. The business that I owned and operated, and loved so much, how much more will I appreciate it, a third time. The ability to sleep in peace, comfortably in a large bed, at home. The freedom to eat what I want, when I want, as well as come and go as I please. Simple freedoms that I took for granted, that most people enjoy on a daily basis.

Losing all these privileges again was a hard lesson to go through. I am learning not to judge people, at least not the way I used to. I have become what I have judged, and despised, a repeat offender, and a loser in the eyes of most, and in society. Most importantly, I have learned that you cannot change other people, or force them to change. As much as you try, and as good as your intentions may be, the simple truth is only that person can make a change themselves.

I learned that while I can help others, and guide them, the only person I can change and must change is myself. I have said before, and I believe firmly in life, we can only do our part. Knowing we have done our part, and gave it our best should bring us peace in the situation at hand. Something I had to again also learn the hard way after losing everything I cared about. I have learned that time is so very precious and how we use can make all the difference in the ultimate outcome of our lives.

I have learned after many mistakes and years of losing in general that breaking the law doesn't solve anything, and by far only creates more problems. If I just stopped to think a few minutes about what I was about to do, look at all the hurt, time, loss, pain and regret I could have saved myself, my family and anyone affected by my poor choices.

I am learning and will continue to learn to accept me for who I am, make changes to better myself, and live for me and my happiness. Also, to accept others for who they are and with their faults too. If I should choose not to like that person, or see what they are harmful to my life, then I simply don't deal with them, and distance myself from them.

A big lesson that I learned in all of this is that I cannot save the world, or any one person, especially one that doesn't want to change or be saved. It is not my job, and only God can have that kind of power to directly save. People are going to be okay with themselves or their lives sometimes, even if everyone around them sees clearly that that person's life is not in order, then again who am I to judge? A big lesson I have learned is not to live in the past, nor dwell on the past.

This is harmful, and when looking to the past I should only look for two reasons. To see what works, and what doesn't work for me and learn from it, turning that failure into something good and positive. The past should be a reminder of what not to do, so when looking back you see more happy memories, therefore live in the present with much less regret. While no one's past is perfect, mind is sure full of poor choices that led me to a lot of painful situations and left me reeling with a lot of regrets.

The future is uncertain at the moment, due to my incarceration, therefore I can only plan so much. While in that planning it has also lead me to a most valuable lesson—one that I am learning all the time. That lesson is to not overwhelm myself, and not to make unrealistic plans, especially too soon. To not try and take on too much, too soon, only adding pressure to my life. This was a huge downfall for me when I was released in February 2018. I was in a hurry to start life and tried playing catch-up. Something you cannot ever do after having any major setback in life, and especially just coming home from prison.

While there are so many lessons I have learned, and I will still learn throughout the course of my life, my object is to make the best of that learning experience, and not subject myself or others to unnecessary, and avoidable pain that comes from poor choices that lead to undesirable places like prison, and unpleasant circumstance as a result of bad decision making. Time is valuable, and time must be taken in decision making and when wanting to live the best, most productive, and happiest life that one can hope to live.

With so many plans made, and so many failures, I have also learned to not skip steps, to lie to myself, to lie to others, and to try and cover or hide a problem for it only to destroy me later. The end result is exactly what happened to me. Lessons can break your heart. They can also build you up and make you much stronger. Throughout this book and my time in prison it has done both. Knowing what you could have and should have done different after the fact is beyond the reason of being too late, it's a torch I no longer want to carry or see anyone suffer from.

So, have I learned? I learned a lot and am still learning lessons every day. Prison will have that effect on you when you sincerely pay attention and want to make a real change for the better. In many painful ways I have learned to be more patient, think before I act, and consider any and all consequences that may follow from one of my choices or decisions that I am going to make.

While healing from the pain and trying to recover from the losses I've endured, I am learning to love myself and so importantly forgive myself. Without both, I cannot move forward in a healthy way, nor will it be possible for me to properly love and forgive others. This is a hard one for me, probably the hardest thing to learn how to do again. It is especially hard to do, to those who have wronged you, or spoke bad about you, but it is necessary if I, or anyone wants to truly heal. There are so many lessons to learn from in life, and my plan, and my hope is to never have to learn a lesson again behind any fences or concrete walls.

These are lessons that can and should be avoided. I am learning to not only love myself, but importantly also respect myself. To respect others, and to respect the law. I could list many more lessons, and I wanted to focus on the big ones. For me, I believe I have done so, and hope anyone reading this can put something in their life into perspective and see a way to learn a valuable lesson from it. The lessons that I've learned will forever play a part in how things could have been, but ultimately where my life can and will go from here.

Lessons learned: 1. Love and respect myself and others. 2. Respect and obey the law. 3. Listen to counsel from family and those who care about me sometimes. 4. Stop and think before you act, and don't be impulsive. 5. Ask for help when needed, and don't be afraid to do so. 6. Take life slow and take on one day at a time as it comes. 7. Don't put high expectations on others only to be disappointed. 8. Accept people for who they are, and don't try to change them. 9. Don't live or dwell in the past. 10. Address your issues and don't cover or run from them. 11. Always be honest with yourself and others. 12. Look back on all these lessons and appreciate all you have learned from them.

CHAPTER 19

# *Truth vs. Lies*

In this corner we have the heavyweight champion. The undefeated, undisputed truth. In the other corner, the challenger. The No. 1 ranked contender, and new way of life, lies. As if the truth or a lie were a boxing match, constantly battling one another. In life a lot of the time we think we can cover the truth with a lie. At first it seems to work, then we have to create another lie. Lie after lie until we have enough lies to cover the truth.

There are jabs thrown, uppercuts, right and left hooks. These are lies. When the truth hits, it's a knockout punch we often don't see coming. The winner and still champion, the truth. For me, I was able to use lies at times to fool others, trying to hide my truth. Seeing that it worked for a time, it appeared to be successful. So much so, that not only could I convince others of my lies, I actually started to believe them myself, and was convinced. I became so convinced it was just easier to lie, and for me safer too.

The fact is, no matter how many lies we try to use to hide the truth it simply doesn't work. You cannot bury something pure; it always comes to the surface. When it does, all the lies are uncovered, leaving damage in its path. Damage to others and to ourselves. The longer we try to hide the truth the more damage it can do, especially in our closest relationships. Remember what I said before about lying to ourselves, who are we trying to fool? Even though the truth hurts sometimes, it's better to deal with the truth and heal, than to discover one's lies and resent them or worse, the person telling the lies.

We lie in fear that we will hurt others, when we actually hurt ourselves. The truth always sets you free by freeing your conscience in knowing you did the right thing being honest, even if you lose something or someone you love in the process. At the very least the truth can be respected, while no one respects a lie. My lies destroyed me, like a hurricane wreaks havoc in its path. The aftermath is a wasteland of damage, and for a person, a mountain of pain to now deal with. If we love one another it's so important to be truthful to each other as well. Lies never protect you, only prevent you from what eventually always reveals itself in time the truth.

The truth is like the light, and a lie is to darkness. Darkness hides from the light, but the light always exposes the darkness for what it truly is. No one wants to be exposed for who they truly are, especially when they lie to cover up big mistakes, or infidelities. We know this to be true. The light doesn't agree with darkness, nor does a lie agree with the truth.

When two people like to each other, now that relationship is built on a foundation of lies, and the initial damage has already begun. For me, this was true. We both lied to one another for our own separate reasons. Neither one of us wound up winning, in a sense that we were both hurt, and the relationship ended with resentment on both sides. All lying to each other did was cause conflict, that caused fights, arguments, lack of trust, and eventual separation.

A lot of pain, and damage could have been spared if we were both truly honest with each other. The common problem we have as humans today is, we all have our own agenda. Our own belief system of what is right, and what is wrong, then followed by what society views as acceptable. While these things may seem true to us, still the truth doesn't care about misplaced beliefs or hidden agendas. The truth has one goal, shedding light on what is real and true. Lies reflect hidden motives and personal agendas to meet our needs in life and fill our selfish pleasures. This is wrong, and just being truthful leaves you feeling better, and it leaves you knowing you were honest. Honestly is still the best policy.

Even little lies can be disastrous when they spread long enough. Another problem with lies being spread is too often people believe them just because many others tell the same lie they heard from someone else. If it started as a lie, it stays a lie. Just because everyone in your circle now gossips about the lie, it doesn't magically make the lie true. Society has long believed what many say, due to numbers and misplaced beliefs, or trying to ride with the train. Integrity is by far one of the greatest qualities any person can possess. It's a solid, truthful foundation to a person and being true to yourself and others at all times.

It may seem difficult, but statistics show that the one single quality that 99% of all billionaires share is their integrity. I have revised what integrity means to me, and I truly believe that this can apply to anyone who wants to have a good name over anything else. Integrity, is remaining the same, being truthful to all parties, even when the circumstances change. It's not something you do or have, just when you think it can benefit you, you do it all the time, because it's the right thing to do!

With my small business, my integrity was always on the line, and this much is true, at least in that aspect of my life I remained honest with my great customers. When all is said and done, how do you want to be remembered? Someone who was honest as trustworthy or have people say you were a fraud, and a liar? I choose my good name, over anything else, in the end, it's all we really have left, and can leave behind spirituality.

Telling the truth can be scary at times, but it serves a greater purpose than one of ourselves and needs. It serves all, so what is true can be known, and we can learn from the truth for our own benefit. Truth vs. lies—the choices that will ultimately shape and decide what direction our lives will take who we will end up with, what we will leave behind, and how we will be remembered.

CHAPTER 20

# *Reflections On Hope For The Future*

There is so much to look back on and remember. There is so much I am learning on this journey as well. Though I wrote a deep chapter about my many regrets, I too can be grateful for this experience to reflect and do a major overhaul of my past life, and with hope looking forward to the next chapter of my life. I think back to how I started my first small business power washing. How I took a used truck with bare minimum starter equipment and built a near six-figure income business in just one short year.

I had so many doubt me, tell me I couldn't succeed in a fallen economy, which at the time was still recovering from the nationwide mortgage crisis in America. I let no negative influence stop me and built my small company into something I was proud to call my own and all the while had also found a way to provide for myself while loving what I was doing. They call that the American dream. Many are in search for it, and some never find it.

It took 33 years of my life to find what I call the stepping-stone—the steppingstone for me in the business world. After losing this business twice, due to the loss of my freedom, I began looking at my other gifts that have been hidden for years. My ability to express myself through writing, and speech along with my business minded skills has taught me to expand my horizon and think bigger. I had already known some super successful people in the world, speaking financially.

In prison, you also meet some people with true stories of their success before they fell and landed themselves in prison. One in particular I would like to briefly share on account of someone I met here in the Philadelphia FDC detention center. Another man who reached great success financially in America, before his fall due to excessive gambling. I could relate, since I lost everything as well due to my gambling addiction that went un-addressed for years.

I met a guy named Vacho who hailed from the great sin city—Las Vegas, Nevada. Here was a guy at just 27 years old who had owned eight businesses. He owned five smoke shops along with three beauty and tanning salons. He said he was making around $80,000 a month on average. Can you imagine earning this much money period, and especially in your twenties. We shared stories of our wild nights out, and our flamboyant lifestyles, and I thought mine were nothing compared to his. I drew this conclusion not based on talent, but mere financial success and material things he had acquired. Like a huge house, and four exotic cars, something a small six-figure earner could barely pull off without being nearly broken afterwards.

The we talked about people who make it in Forbes Magazine and which are usually considered the most successful people around the world. It made me reflect on two big things. One, how bad gambling can destroy anyone, even the richest person in the world. Two, how much un-tapped potential I really had and could still use in order to prosper again and at a much higher level than before. My past is filled with mini-success stories and yet filled with just as many failures. How so, simply because I put more of my energy into negative ideas than into positive ones.

Wasted time is the end result, and something I intend not to do anymore. As I sit incarcerated reflecting on so many things, I also look at how I can make time for myself as well as being a work-a-holic, because making time for yourself is essential if you truly want to find happiness as well. You could say everything in moderation. You could also say the ability to manage all areas of your life. I had always considered myself a multi-tasker, but I often drifted off to negative ideas and such destructive hobbies, such as gambling, a true loser's game.

After losing so much, including time and excessive amounts of money, it has brought me to this conclusion. There is no more time to waste. A famous quote states that, 'You either build your dream, or someone else will hire you to build theirs.' This hit me and made me want to explore my un-tapped potential like never before. Something I am limited to do at the moment, but will surely do upon my release from prison, and for the final time. There has been an overwhelming amount of reflection into so many areas of my life. Financial failures, my gambling addiction, failed relationships, and business prospects that I have yet to begin to explore and put into serious action, from day to day, with expectations that we will reach whatever goals or things we are searching for or trying to accomplish.

What I forgot to implement—which was so crucial—was some real much-needed me time, just to enjoy and appreciate life with all it has to offer. A simple one week vacation flying away somewhere far from home and all the cares and responsibilities would have done me so much good and gave me a chance to slow down and not move so fast as I was trying to do, before my last big fall. Still, I have hope. The show is not over, and when I return home this time, enjoying my freedom will be a requirement for my plan of success and ultimately my happiness.

I expect to be somewhere in my 40's, hopefully early ones and will use my experiences as a former small businessman, and all the lessons I learned from my past mistakes to better shape my plans for the future, with a greater hope, and also things I can and will learn in prison, especially how to expand not only my former business, but grow as an entrepreneur too. There is much work to be done, and I look forward to doing the work necessary.

I will not stop there. Building my relationship with God also has great meaning to me, and seeing the world not just through a businessman's eyes, but spiritual eyes as well. I plan to use time and make it work for me, and stop allowing it to work against me, as I have done so much in the past. I want my family to see a real change in me, and again someday make my mother proud of me. I want to be that example for hope and real change. Not just us a financial platform to enjoy the finer things in life. A message shared is truly priceless, and what I have set out to achieve.

I believe everyone has some message they would like to share in their lifetime, no matter how big or small it may seem. We all have that right, and also that ability if we try hard enough. Effort is vital in anything, and time is so precious. In my reflections, I have thought if I could only turn back time 10 years ago, and know what I know now, how different things could have been. Today, I say to myself 10 years from now I want to look back saying I did what I set out to do, with little regret, no second thoughts and left a good example that anyone can follow.

Along with other formulas I attribute to success, by far this would be one of them. Looking back with no regrets. Easier said than done, some say, but not impossible. Knowing I at least tried and made real efforts to achieve my goals by taking action and not just talking about it, achieves that very goal. Nothing can change the past I lived, but history doesn't have to repeat itself. This is my hope for the future. My dreams can become reality by shifting all that negative energy I once wasted on meaningless things, and focusing it on building something positive, productive, meaningful and enjoyable to me all at the same time.

That, my friends, can be truly successful and a story I hope I can share someday. Reflecting on the past— good or bad times— puts into great perspective what we truly want out of life, before the show is all over. Some of us get there, and some of us don't. The only difference between the two are resources, or some sort of freak luck, it's the effort and the plan of action we take that will bring us to our destination.

I have my boarding ticket and I am ready to fly. My destination may still be unknown geographically, but internally and outwardly I intend it to be a success. Having the peace of mind, and within that

I have searched for most of my life and being able to do the things I want to do, enjoying them with the people that I love.

If anything I have written one can relate to, I am sure the last topic mentioned is one that all of us would want and like to achieve in their lifetime. Maybe some of you have already, and you can count yourselves lucky and very fortunate if you have reached that destination. Not every plane you get on is going to take you there, and there may be detours or roadblocks along the way. Do not give up, and always take some time to reflect on what you truly want out of your life.

Then ask yourself, have you arrived yet? I cannot say how long the flight or journey may be, but it's one trip I am excited to take and enjoy. If you made it thus far, and shared my pain, felt my deep regrets, or may have experienced similar losses, my heart is with you. There is hope. Time to change and make a difference and start enjoying life to its fullest. The decision is yours to make, and yours alone. While others may encourage us, only we can motivate yourself and put in the required effort and work to make our life what we want it to be.

So, through theses true confessions, I have learned a lot, and I have shared my experiences. I hope that all my readers may gain something from it too. Thank you all for listening and reading my story. My story ends here for now, but in my many reflections, with hope for the future. My final message here is no dream or goal is too big, if you want it bad enough!

The End

# *Closing note*

The truth is, when I first started writing this book, my initial intent was to vent, express my pain, regrets, failures, and speak of my losses and share the wrongs I felt I endured. As I continued to write, I dug deeper into my own truth, and saw a way to use my true confessions as examples for my readers, with hope that they could learn from, and identify their own truth. The truth can set us all free when we are honest with ourselves as well as one another. I want to thank all of you for allowing me the chance to share with you my true confessions and hope you learned something as well as enjoyed reading my book.

Thank you all,
Michael Fanelli